Book 2

SPELLING SUCCESS

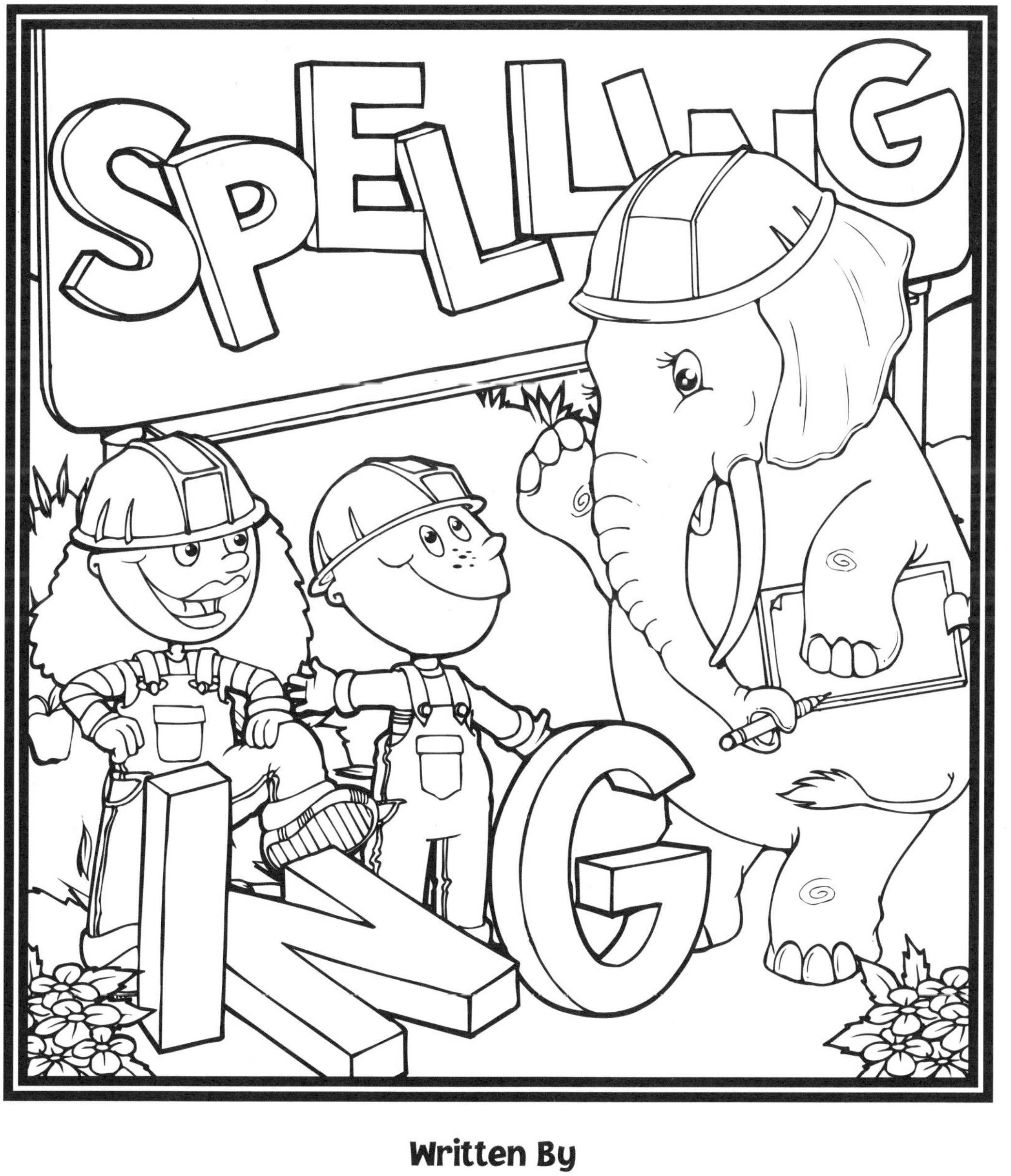

Written By

Jenny Nitert and Debra Salerno

Published By

World Teachers Press®

Published with the permission of R.I.C. Publications Pty. Ltd.

First published by R.I.C. Publications Pty. Ltd., Perth, Western Australia. Revised by Didax Educational Resources.

Distributed in Canada by Scholar's Choice.

Printed in the United States of America.

Order Number 2-5150
ISBN 1-58324-077-2

B C D E F 03 02

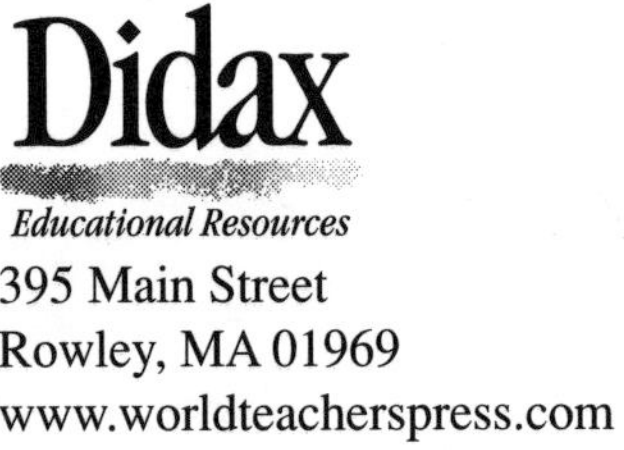

395 Main Street
Rowley, MA 01969
www.worldteacherspress.com

Foreword

Spelling Success *is a comprehensive, whole-year program providing you with a solid framework to develop independent spellers.*

The aim of the series is to take students back to basics when learning to spell. Each list has been compiled to support this approach with words from proven contemporary lists. These words were chosen to reflect the students' language abilities, interests and experiences.

Students are encouraged, by way of a focus, to discover for themselves key features, patterns, rules, similarities and differences within each list. The variety of activities accompanying each list provides students with the opportunity to use different strategies to consolidate the focus.

Detailed explanations and program outlines have been provided to ensure maximum use and value of the program. Overview lists from the previous year have been included to make review easy, along with dictation sentences for you to incorporate into the regular spelling program.

Evaluation has been made easy by the inclusion of a teacher checklist and student certificates. Space for student self-evaluation has also been incorporated at the conclusion of each list.

Contents

Teachers Notes

Each list contains two pages. The first page is designed to give the students as much practice looking at and writing the list words as possible, while the second page is designed as a word building and word study page. An outline of how to best use the pages is shown below.

The **list words** are grouped according to:

- phonic groups;
- word families;
- phonic families;
- commonly used words; or
- contractions.

This **focus** is designed to encourage students to look for patterns, similarities or differences within the list.

Students are also asked to underline the key features – this helps them to focus on important parts or features of the list words.

List One **Spelling Success**

ship wish
shop dish
shut fish
shin brush
sheep smash

Look at the words.
Say each word.
Underline the pattern.

The pattern is ☐☐ *at the beginning or end of each word.*

1. Fill in the missing vowels to complete the list words.

sh ___ ___ p f ___ sh
w ___ sh sm ___ sh
br ___ sh sh ___ n
sh ___ t sh ___ p
sh ___ p
d ___ sh

2. Word Hunt

Which list words rhyme?

Which list words have five letters?

Which list words have four letters and end in "p"?

Your notebook

1. Write the **List One** words using – look, say, cover, write, check.
2. Write five more **sh** words. Check the spelling.
3. Write **My List** words using – look, say, cover, write, check.
4. Find small words in **My List** words.

- 16 - *Spelling Success–Book 2* *World Teachers Press®*

Your Notebook activities are designed to be completed over several days in the students' spelling notebooks. Their aim is to provide students with several opportunities to write both the list words and their personal list words and to use them in various ways.

These **activities** are designed to provide many opportunities for students to complete or write the list words.

On this page you will find:

- secret words;
- word shapes;
- missing letters;
- unjumbles;
- word searches;
- backwards words; or
- rhyming words.

Teachers Notes Continued

The second page is designed to extend and develop students' knowledge and understanding of the word list.

List One — **Spelling Success**

3. Find small words in these List One words.

ship ______ shop ______ shut ______

shin ______ sheep ______ ______

4. Use the List One words to complete the sentences.

(a) Please ______ the door.

(b) A baby ______ is a lamb.

(c) A ______ lives in water.

(d) He sailed across the ocean on a ______ .

5. Add "s" to these words to make them say more than one.

ship ______ shop ______

shin ______

6. Add "es" to these words to make them say more than one.

wish ______

dish ______

brush ______

My List

clubhouse

Make a Book

1. Use paper to make a book.
2. Write a word from both lists on each page until all words have been used.
3. Draw a picture for each.

World Teachers Press® Spelling Success–Book 2 - 17 -

On this page you will find:

1. **Word Study** - various activities covering antonyms, synonyms and homonyms are developed from the list to give students a broader knowledge of words that follow a pattern or fit into a category.
2. **Word Building** - practice for students is provided to allow them to build on and create a larger bank of words for their use and understanding.
3. **Interesting Facts** - these have been included to encourage students to have a deeper awareness of words and language and how it works.
4. **Notebook Activities** - further activities to be completed in the students' spelling notebooks as part of the daily spelling program.

Rules - explanations, examples and activities are designed to teach students why words look the way they do, why they are spelled the way they are and exceptions to rules.

Students are encouraged to incorporate **personal words** within the spelling program.

These words can be obtained from:

- the students' writing;
- common errors;
- previous spelling errors from list words;
- theme words;
- topic words from science, mathematics, or other subject areas; or
- reading words.

The **face** allows students to evaluate how they feel they handled this list.

The **clubhouse** activities have been incorporated into the book as a form of extension and/or conclusion to the list.

Through an interesting craft activity or game, students are able to consolidate the words from the word list and their own list.

Suggested Timetable

Lists One to Twenty each cover a two-week period and progress in level of difficulty through the book.

While activities have been provided to consolidate the focus of each list, an eclectic teaching approach is desirable to ensure spelling remains an interesting challenge.

A suggested daily program for the two-week spelling period has been outlined below as a guide to how the program works. These lessons have been developed based on a 25-minute lesson. You may wish to add to or delete from the program according to the time frame that works for your class.

DAY ONE
- Pretest List One and introduce list words
- Encourage students to discover the focus
- Underline the key features
- Select personal list words and transfer list words to Journal Page (*Journal Page, p14*)
- Complete Activity One

DAY TWO
- Spelling game (*Class or Group Games, p11*)
- Review the focus for this list
- Complete remaining first page activities
- Complete Activity One from *Your Notebook*

DAY THREE
- Class Test
- Make word shapes for each spelling word and swap with a partner (*Individual Activities, p10*)
- Complete Activity Two from *Your Notebook*

DAY FOUR
- Make "What am I?" clues for each spelling word and swap with a partner (*Individual Activities, p10)*
- Complete any remaining activities in *Your Notebook*

DAY FIVE
- Class Test
- Spelling game or activity *(Spelling Activities, p10–11)*
- Dictation sentences *(Dictation Sentences, p9)*

DAY SIX
- Review the focus for this list
- Brainstorm other words that follow the focus
- Spelling game or activity *(Spelling Activities, p10–11)*

DAY SEVEN
- Class Test
- Separate the activities on page two - do one per day for the remainder of the program
- Spelling game or activity *(Spelling Activities, p10-11)*

DAY EIGHT
- Complete one page two activity
- Spelling game or activity *(Spelling Activities, p10-11)*

DAY NINE
- Class Test
- Complete one page two activity
- Start *Clubhouse* activity
- Dictation sentences *(Dictation Sentences, p9)*

DAY TEN
- Complete *Clubhouse* activity
- Review of list words
- Post test

Preparation

*A **Journal Page** has been provided on page 14 for photocopying. It is suggested that each student be given a new copy of the Journal Page at the commencement of the new list. This provides the student with a method of recording how he or she is learning the words in each list.*

*The **Clubhouse** activities require some preparation, but provided the basics are kept on hand, preparation is kept to a minimum. Some items you will need:*

- flashcards
- glue
- modeling clay
- string
- hole punch
- calculators
- cardboard
- sand/glitter
- scissors
- pipe cleaners
- stapler
- markers/highlighters
- colored/plain paper
- colored pencils/crayons
- grid/graph paper
- coat hangers
- containers of various sizes
- scrap paper

Overview

List	Main Focus	Additional Focus	✓/X
1	Initial **sh–** and final **–sh**	Small Words, Sentences, Adding **–s** and Adding **–es**	
2	Initial **ch–** and final **–ch**	Sentences, Plural Words and Small Words	
3	**a – e** and **i – e**	Unjumble Sentences, Rule – Adding **–ing**	
4	**o – e** and **u – e**	Sentences, Adding Suffixes	
5	Initial **dr–**, **gr–**, **tr–**, **br–** and **cr–**	Sentences – Singular and Plural, Rule – Adding **–es** to words ending in **–y**	
6	Initial **st–** and final **–st**	Sentences – Tense, Plural Words, Antonyms	
7	Initial **sk–**, **sp–** and **sw–**	Rule – Adding **–ing**, Doubling Final Letter, Synonyms	
8	Final **–nt** and **–mp**	Unjumble Sentences, Adding **–ed**	
9	**ea**, **ee** and **ear**	Sentences, Homophones, Adding **–er** and **–es**, Synonyms	
10	Commonly Used Words	Sentences, Fill in the Blanks, Adding **–ed**	
11	**–ang**, **–ong**, **–ing** and **–ung**	Adding **–er**, Compound Words, Small Words	
12	Same Sound **ay** and **ai**	Homophones, Sentences, Adding **–ed**	
13	Same Sound **ir**, **er** and **ur**	Antonyms, Syllabification	
14	Same Sound **oa** and **ow**	Answer Yes/No, Rule – Change **f** to **v** when adding **–es**, Adding Suffixes	
15	Commonly Used Words	Sentences – Capital Letters, Homophones, Fill in the Blanks	
16	Same Sound **ou** and **ow**	Unjumble Sentences, Syllables, Antonyms	
17	Final **–y**	Small Words, Rule – Adding **–es** to words ending in **–y**, Synonyms	
18	Initial **wh–** and **w–**	Sentences – Capital Letters, Small Words	
19	Initial **th–** and final **–th**	Sentences – Plurals, Alphabetical Order, Rhyming Words, Hard and Soft **th**	
20	Contractions	Contraction Sort, Forming Contractions	

List Words

Book One List Words

List Eleven	can, man, ran, fan, pan
List Twelve	vet, met, net, wet, pet
List Thirteen	win, fin, pin, tin, bin
List Fourteen	cot, hot, dot, tot, pot
List Fifteen	hug, rug, jug, mug, bug
List Sixteen	has, ten, big, dog, nut
List Seventeen	had, yes, did, got, bus
List Eighteen	Dad, bed, dig, box, Mom
List Nineteen	be, he, me, we, she
List Twenty	my, fly, by, sky, cry
List Twenty-One	see, meet, feet, need, tree, feed, seed, seen
List Twenty-Two	moon, food, room, soon, boot, roof, zoo, noon
List Twenty-Three	and, hand, sand, land, band, end, bend, send
List Twenty-Four	all, ball, call, small, took, book, look, cook
List Twenty-Five	into, the, him, her, was, get, one, but

Book Two List Words

List One	ship, shop, shut, shin, sheep, wish, dish, fish, brush, smash
List Two	chop, chip, chin, chick, chest, rich, such, each, lunch, much
List Three	gave, take, make, made, came, like, ride, kite, five, time
List Four	home, bone, note, those, woke, use, tube, cute, tune, cube
List Five	drum, drip, grip, grub, trip, try, bring, brave, crab, crib
List Six	stop, stone, stand, start, step, nest, must, lost, best, cost
List Seven	skip, skin, spot, spade, spell, spin, swim, swing, sweep, sweet
List Eight	tent, spent, ant, hint, plant, camp, lamp, jump, bump, lump
List Nine	meat, teach, beach, leave, dear, near, fear, keep, sleep, sheet
List Ten	for, were, going, help, come, ask, you, said, give, from
List Eleven	bang, hang, sang, song, along, sing, thing, being, sung, hung
List Twelve	day, way, play, clay, away, rain, train, sail, tail, wait
List Thirteen	bird, girl, first, third, hurt, turn, paper, never, over, under
List Fourteen	boat, coat, loaf, float, soap, grow, show, below, own, crow
List Fifteen	does, put, once, goes, why, some, done, are, here, saw
List Sixteen	out, about, house, found, around, now, how, brown, down, clown
List Seventeen	story, lady, baby, party, only, happy, bunny, funny, silly, very
List Eighteen	when, what, where, while, whip, well, went, with, will, want
List Nineteen	them, this, then, they, that, than, both, tooth, path, bath
List Twenty	I'm, isn't, he's, she's, I'll, don't, can't, it's, we're, I've

Dictation Sentences

List One	I wish I was on a ship. The fish shop door is shut. The vet shut the sheep in the room.
List Two	I wish to be rich. The chick looked in the chest for seed. We each had fish and chips for lunch.
List Three	I can fly a kite. Mom gave me five chicks. I like to ride my bike all the time.
List Four	I gave my dog a bone at home. Those small chicks are cute. I will use those cubes to fill the tube.
List Five	I took a trip to get a drum. I will try to be brave. The crab had a big grub for lunch.
List Six	I can step on the stone. I lost my best book under the stand. The chick must be in the nest.
List Seven	The food was sweet. My skin has spots on it. I can spin on my swing while I spell.
List Eight	An ant is on the plant. We can camp in my tent. I jump on the lumps in my bed.
List Nine	I sleep under my sheet. We took a tent to the beach to keep cool. He had to leave the crab at the beach.
List Ten	Did you ask for help? He is going home to sleep. We were going to ask you to come to the beach.
List Eleven	I can sing along to the song. He can bang the drum and sing. We sang a sweet song for Mom and Dad.
List Twelve	We will sail away. I like to play with clay. We had to wait all day for the train.
List Thirteen	The bird was hurt. Turn the paper over. Did you come first or third in the race?
List Fourteen	The soap did not float. The fish swims below the boat. I will show you my coat with spots on it.
List Fifteen	Why does the boat float? I once saw a crow in a boat. Why did some of the clay pots break?
List Sixteen	I saw about five boats out on the water. The first clown fell down. We found a brown bird in the house.
List Seventeen	The baby is very happy. The funny clown will come to the party. In the story, the lady had a funny bunny.
List Eighteen	What will you sing at the party? When will the baby come home? The chips went well with the fish for lunch.
List Nineteen	I lost my tooth in the bath. That girl fell on the path and was hurt. Both the girls said they would come to the party.
List Twenty	I'm happy I found my tooth. She's a funny clown. I can't go into the shop when it's closed.

Spelling Activities

The following activities and games have been provided for your use as additional support to the spelling program. They are a guide and can be developed to suit any class, small group, individual student, teaching program, or teaching style.

Choose from the following activities and games if not already covered in the particular list being used.

Individual Activities

Useful for developing familiarity with the list words.

- Make word shapes, word snakes, or word problems for spelling words.
- Find small words in list words.
- Write rhyming words for the spelling words.
- Write the list words in alphabetical order.
- Write spelling words with eyes closed or from memory.
- Sort words according to: initial/final letters, number of letters, number of syllables, number of vowels, number of consonants, parts of speech, or by student's own choice.
- Find antonyms, synonyms, homophones, or homographs for the spelling words.
- Make word builders by adding **s**, **ed**, **ing**, **er**, **est**.
- Rank words from easiest to most difficult to spell or vice versa.
- Write definitions for spelling words.
- Make fold-up books containing spelling words.

Partner Activities

Develops cooperation and increases knowledge of list words.

- Make "What am I?" clues.
- Make an alphabet search using list words.
- Make read and draw activities and swap with a partner.
- Jumble words and swap with a partner.
- Jumble sentences using spelling words and swap with a partner.
- Make simple word searches on graph paper and swap with a partner.
- Make yes/no questions containing spelling words and swap with a partner.

Shared Group Activities

Encourages the exchange of personal list words, therefore, broadening the individual student's word base.

- Make a word bank of words following the same sound or pattern, as individuals, partners, small groups, or whole class.
- Put spelling words into sentences – individually or as a whole class.

Spelling Activities Continued

Class or Group Games

Useful for the reinforcement of the list words in a less formal approach.

- Hold simple class spelling competitions.
- Use individual books, charts, shared stories, or poems to find a particular spelling pattern or rule being studied.
- Play snap, concentration, fish, or word bingo.
- Play tic tac toe using visual patterns or sound patterns to match words.
- Play hangman where students need to guess the letters in the word.
- Guess my word – students ask questions that require a yes/no response to guess the mystery spelling word.

Clubhouse Activities

Useful for the reinforcement of the list words in a less formal approach.

- Make and illustrate booklets.
- Make bookmarks with spelling words.
- Make word mobiles.
- Make modeling clay or pipe cleaner spelling words.
- Make sand or glitter spelling words.
- Paint spelling words.
- Write spelling words in the shape of a list word.
- Do a magazine hunt for spelling words.
- Trace spelling words on partner's back – partner guesses which spelling word was traced.
- Use bright colors to trace spelling words.

Word Study

A range of blackline masters published by World Teachers Press® are available to support the word study component of this spelling program.

Evaluation Suggestions

Evaluation for each list begins with a pretest of the list words before the students see the list words. This can be used as a benchmark for how well the students learn the list or which words they need to focus on throughout the two-week program.

If appropriate, students can then complete a partner test each day and record their results on their Journal Page. If not, students can be tested every other day by you as a whole class.

A post test is then required at the conclusion of the two-week program to evaluate the students' progress. Problem words are recorded and transferred, ready for their personal list in the next list of words to be studied.

It is recommended that review tests are incorporated into the program on a regular basis to ensure previous list words are kept current in the students' memories.

Two recording formats have been included. Format one allows for the recording of each test each student takes, while format two allows for easy recording and follow-up of individual words in each list. This allows for flexibility and accountability within the spelling program. It also allows you to easily evaluate each student or the whole class on two different levels of achievement.

Test Checklist

List ______________ List ______________

Student Name	Pre test	T1	T2	T3	T4	Post test	Pre test	T1	T2	T3	T4	Post test	Review

Spelling Matrix

List ____________

Student name / Words										

How you can become a better speller…

1. **Write It!**
   Write the word on a piece of paper. Does it look right? If it doesn't look right, try spelling it another way.
2. **Break the word into parts.**
   Clap the syllables, say each part quietly in your head, then write the word in its parts.
3. **Look around your classroom.**
   There are probably many words around you that you just didn't notice.
4. **Ask the teacher.**
   If you have tried the first three, then ask your teacher for help.

Look
Say
Cover
Write
Check

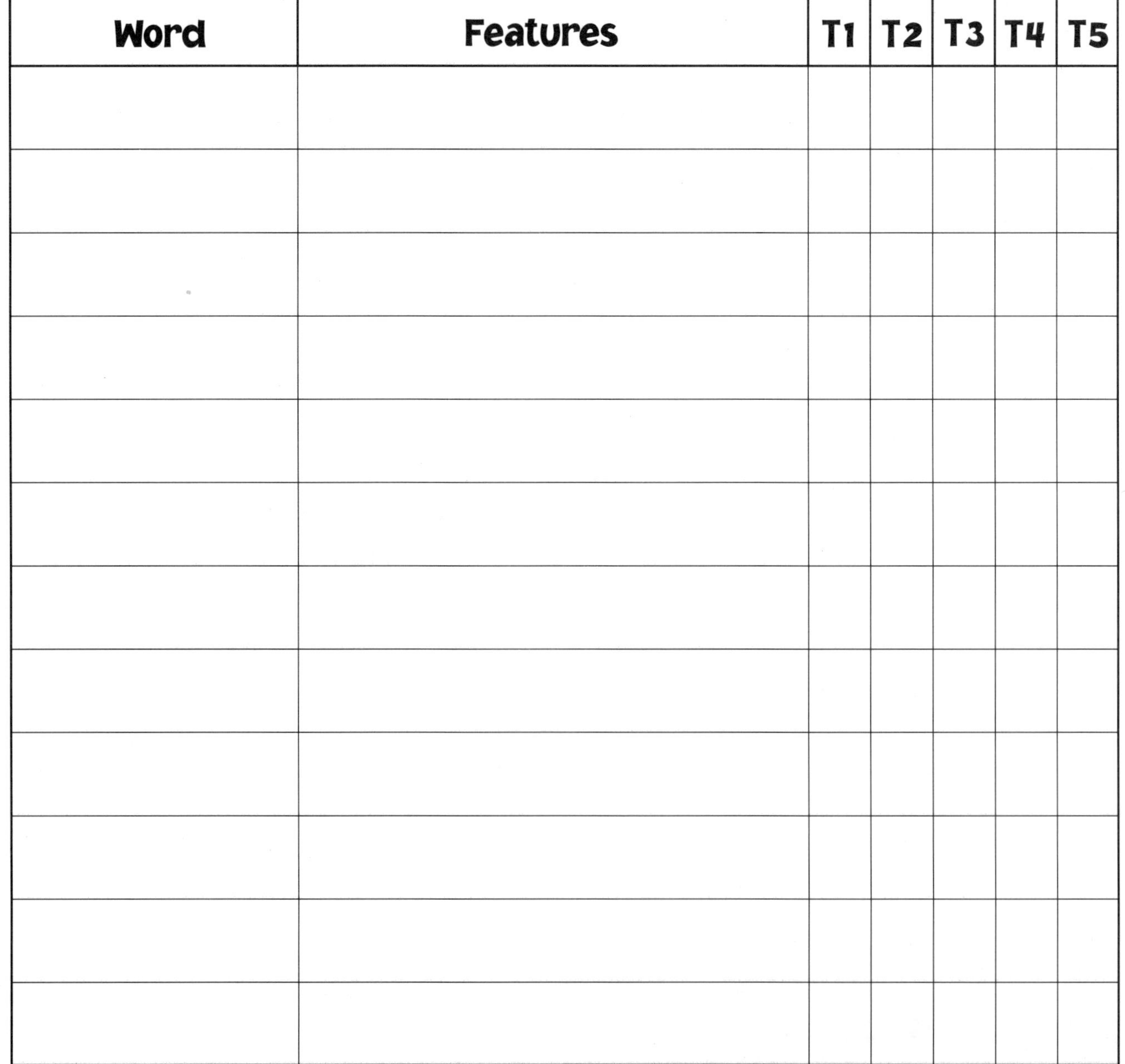

Word	Features	T1	T2	T3	T4	T5

CONGRATULATIONS

Spelling Award

for

Signed Date

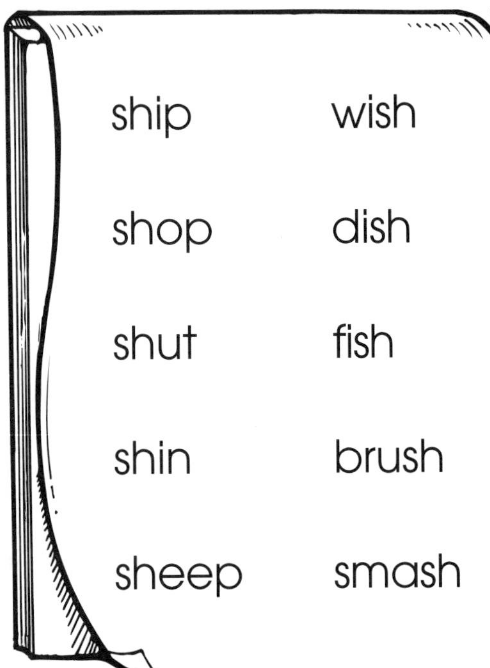

Look at the words.
Say each word.
Underline the pattern.

The pattern is ☐☐ *at the beginning or end of each word.*

1. **Fill in the missing vowels to complete the list words.**

sh ____ ____ p   f ____ sh

w ____ sh   sm ____ sh

br ____ sh   sh ____ n

sh ____ t   sh ____ p

sh ____ p

d ____ sh

2. **Word Hunt**

Which list words rhyme?

____

____

____

Which list words have five letters?

____

____

____

Which list words have four letters and end in "p"?

______________ ______________

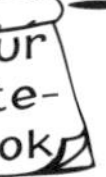

1. Write the **List One** words using – look, say, cover, write, check.
2. Write five more **sh** words. Check the spelling.
3. Write **My List** words using – look, say, cover, write, check.
4. Find small words in **My List** words.

3. Find small words in these List One words.

ship ______ shop ______ shut ______

shin ______ sheep ______ ______

4. Use the List One words to complete the sentences.

(a) Please ______ the door.

(b) A baby ______ is a lamb.

(c) A ______ lives in water.

(d) He sailed across the ocean on a ______ .

5. Add "s" to these words to make them say more than one.

ship ______ shop ______

shin ______

6. Add "es" to these words to make them say more than one.

wish ______

dish ______

brush ______

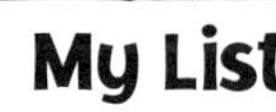

My List

______

______

______

______

______

clubhouse

Make a Book

1. Use paper to make a book.
2. Write a word from both lists on each page until all words have been used.
3. Draw a picture for each.

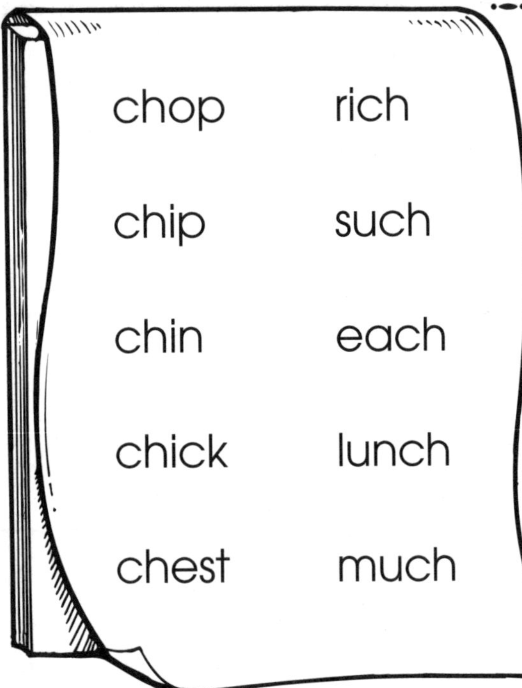

Look at the words.
Say each word.
Underline the pattern.

The pattern is  *at the beginning or end of each word.*

1. Fill in the missing vowels to complete the list words.

____ ____ ch

ch ____ p

r ____ ch

ch ____ ck

m ____ ch

ch ____ st

s ____ ch

ch ____ n

l ____ nch

ch ____ p

2. Unjumble the list words.

poch ______________

icrh ______________

humc ______________

ucsh ______________

chea ______________

pich ______________

3. Guess the list word by its shape.

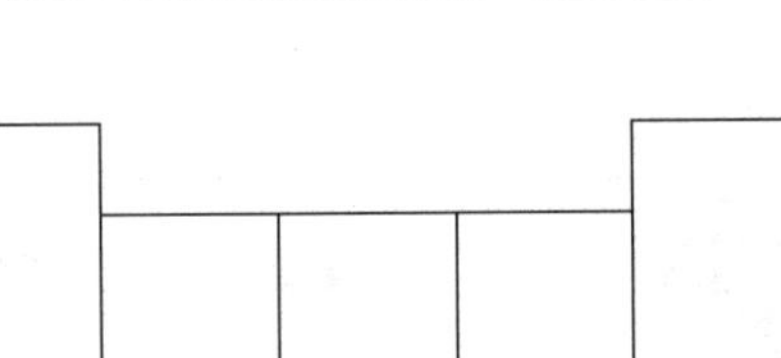

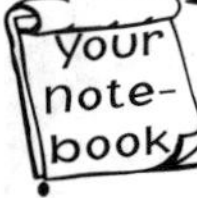

1. Write the **List Two** words using – look, say, cover, write, check.
2. Write five more **ch** words. Check the spelling.
3. Write **My List** words using – look, say, cover, write, check.
4. Make word shapes for each **My List** word.

4. Use the List Two words to complete the sentences.

(a) It was ____________ a hot day.

(b) Give a book to ____________ child.

(c) How ____________ does it cost?

(d) The little ____________ was fluffy and yellow.

5. Look at each picture. Circle the correct word. Write it on the line.

chick, chicks ____________

____________ lunch, lunches

chest, chests ____________

6. Find small words in these List Two words.

chop ____________

chip ____________

chin ____________

clubhouse

Pipe Cleaner Words

Use pipe cleaners to make the words from both lists.

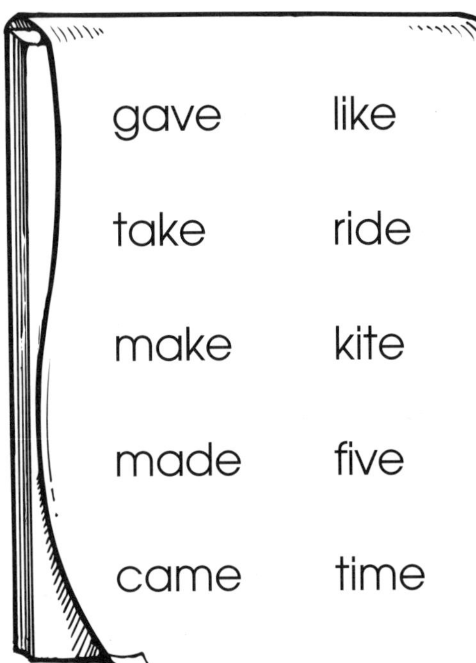

Look at the words.
Say each word.
Underline the patterns.

The patterns are ☐ – ☐ *and* ☐ – ☐ .

The "e" makes the vowel sound long.

1. Write "a–e" or "i–e" to complete the list words.

m ___ d ___   k ___ t ___

t ___ m ___   g ___ v ___

c ___ m ___   m ___ k ___

l ___ k ___   r ___ d ___

f ___ v ___   t ___ k ___

2. Write a list word that rhymes with these.

game ______________

bike ______________

hive ______________

save ______________

shade ______________

3. What am I?

I can fly.
I don't have wings.
I have a long string and a tail.

I am a ______________ .

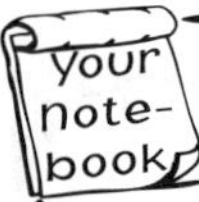

1. Write the **List Three** words using – look, say, cover, write, check.
2. Choose five list words and write each in a sentence.
3. Write **My List** words using – look, say, cover, write, check.
4. Write a rhyming word for each **My List** word.

4. Unjumble the sentences. Circle the List Three words.

(a) you. Take with book the

(b) bike? you ride Can a

(c) is What time? the

(d) can bed. my I make

"e" goes away
when "ing" comes to stay.
For example, take – taking.

5. Add "ing" to these list words.

make ____________

ride ____________

time ____________

My List

Accordion Words

1. Fold long strips of paper like an accordion.
2. Write the words from both lists on the strips.
3. Cut the strips at the end of each word.

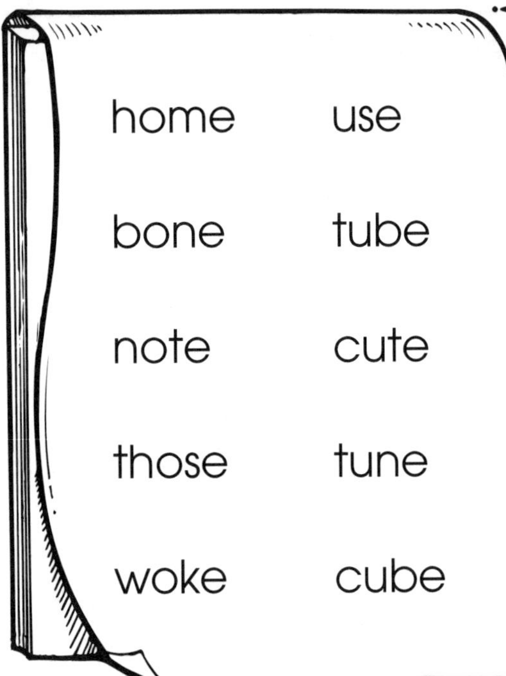

Look at the words.
Say each word.
Underline the pattern.

The patterns are  *and*

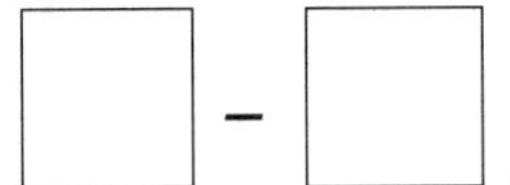 *.*

Th "e" makes the vowel sound long.

1. **Write "o–e" or "u–e" to complete the list words.**

____ s ____   th ____ s ____

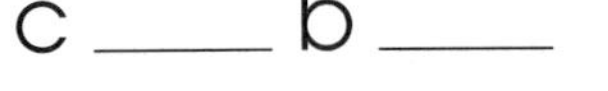

c ____ b ____   t ____ n ____

b ____ n ____   h ____ m ____

t ____ b ____   n ____ t ____

w ____ k ____   c ____ t ____

2. **Word Hunt**

Write the shortest and the longest list word.

____

____

Which list words rhyme?

____

____

Write the list word that means the same.

house ______________

pipe ______________

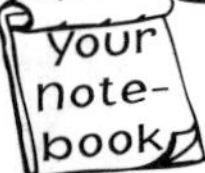

1. Write the **List Four** words using – look, say, cover, write, check.
2. Choose five list words and write each in a sentence.
3. Write **My List** words using – look, say, cover, write, check.
4. Make spelling problems for each **My List** word. For example, ho + me = home.

3. Choose the correct List Four word.

(a) The kitten has a (note, cute, tune) ________________ face.

(b) I (cube, those, woke) ________________ up at six o'clock.

(c) My dog loves to chew on a

(home, bone, tube) ________________ .

(d) My sister wrote a (note, bone, cube)

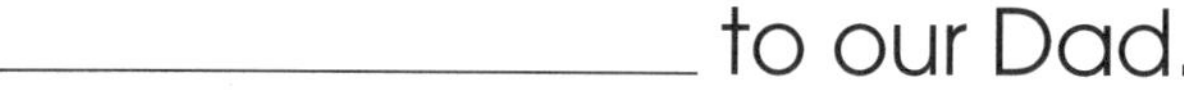 to our Dad.

4. The word "bones" is made from bone.
From which list words are these words made?
Circle the letters that have been added.

used ________________

notes ________________

woken ________________

cubes ________________

using ________________

clubhouse

Mobile

Make a mobile of the **List Four** words and **My List** words.

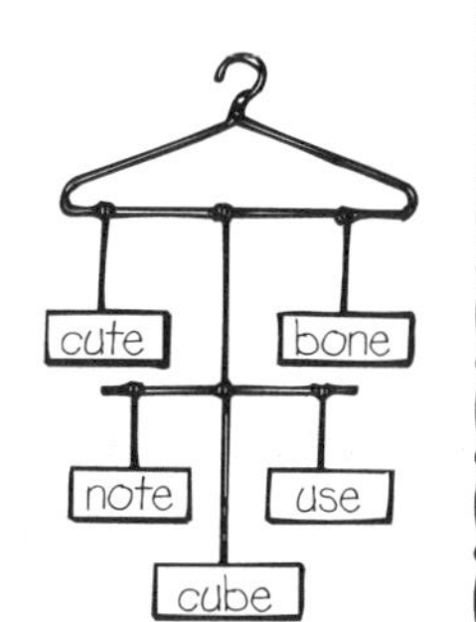

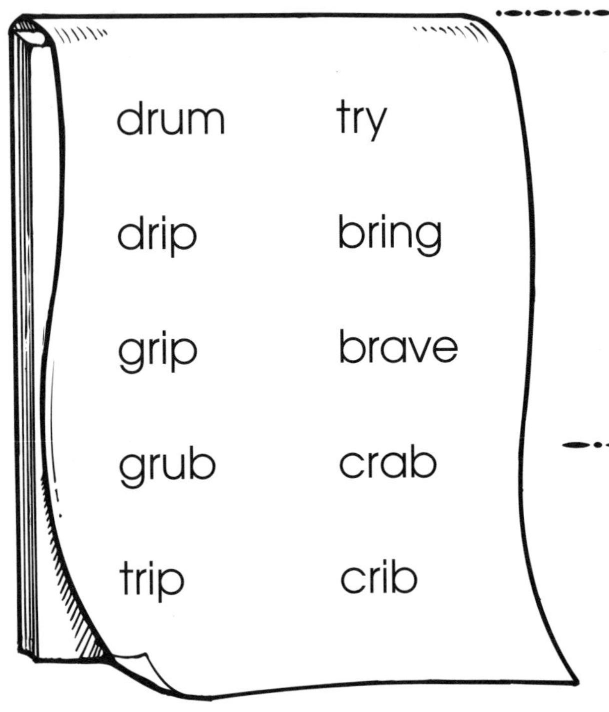

Look at the words.
Say each word.
Underline the pattern.

The words begin with ☐ *r,* ☐ *r,* ☐ *r,* ☐ *r and* ☐ *r.*

1. **Write the correct beginning for each list word.**

____ ____ ub ____ ____ ib

____ ____ um ____ ____ ip

____ ____ ing ____ ____ ip

____ ____ ip ____ ____ y

____ ____ ab

____ ____ ave

2. **Secret Words**

Add "d" to the start of rip.

____

Add "c" to the start of rib.

____

Add "b" to the start of ring.

____

Take "s" off save and put in "br."

____

Take "sk" off sky and put in "tr."

____

Your note-book

1. Write the **List Five** words using – look, say, cover, write, check.
2. Write a rhyming word for each **List Five** word.
3. Write **My List** words using – look, say, cover, write, check.
4. Write **My List** words in alphabetical order.

3. Choose the correct word.

   (a) We went on a (trip, trips) ____________ to the park.

   (b) When you bang on a (drum, drums) ____________ it makes a loud noise.

   (c) Dad found many (grub, grubs) ____________ eating the small plants.

   (d) (Crab, Crabs) ____________ can be caught in a net.

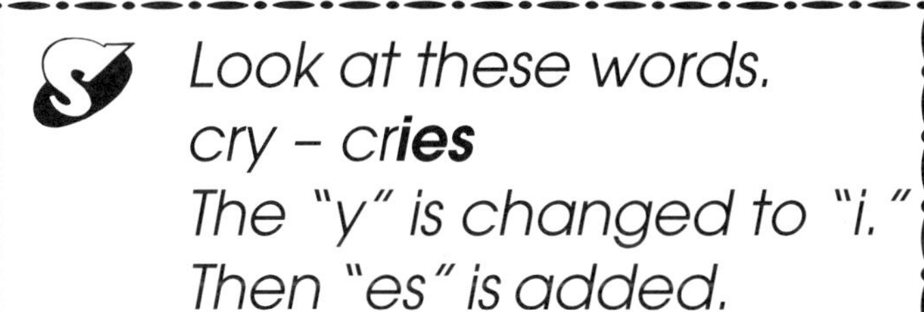

Look at these words.
*cry – cr**ies***
The "y" is changed to "i."
Then "es" is added.

4. Do the same to these words.

try ____________

dry ____________

fry ____________

fly ____________

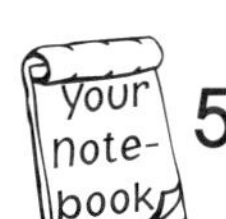

5. Write each new word from Activity 4 in a sentence.

Make a Jigsaw Puzzle

1. Collect blank flashcards.

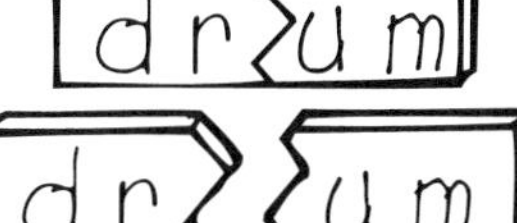

2. Write each word from both lists on a card.

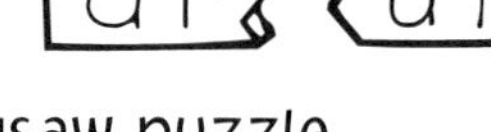

3. Cut each card into a jigsaw puzzle.

Look at the words.
Say each word.
Underline the pattern.

The pattern is ☐☐ *at the beginning or end of each word.*

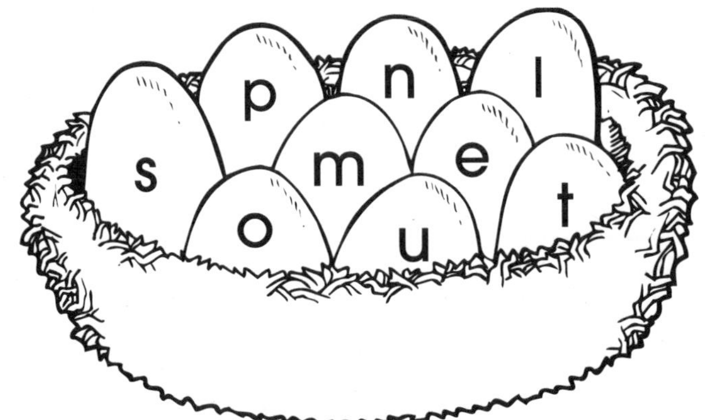

1. Fill in the missing vowels to complete the list words.

st ____ rt   b ____ st

l ____ st   st ____ nd

c ____ st   st ____ n ____

st ____ p   n ____ st

m ____ st   st ____ p

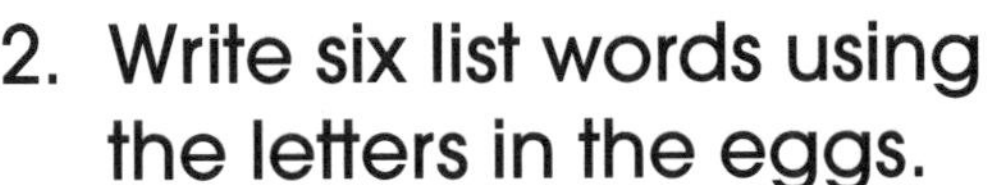

2. Write six list words using the letters in the eggs.

____

____

____

____

____

____

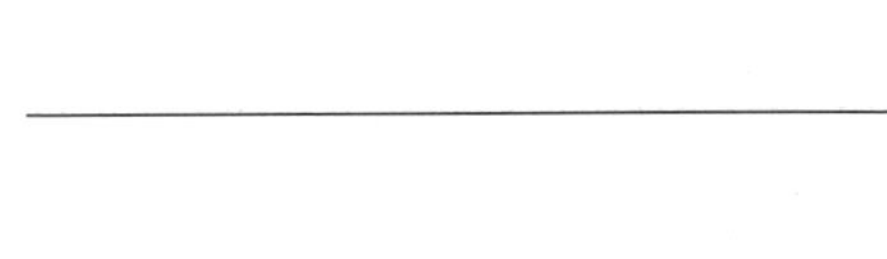

Your note-book

1. Write the **List Six** words using – look, say, cover, write, check.
2. Write a rhyming word for each **List Six** word.
3. Write **My List** words using – look, say, cover, write, check.
4. Write each **My List** word in a sentence.

3. Choose the correct word.

(a) "Please (stop, stopped) ______________ talking," said the teacher.

(b) Our car (stop, stopped) ______________ at the red light.

(c) The puppet show will (start, started) ______________ in five minutes.

(d) It (started, start) ______________ to rain very hard.

4. Make these words say more than one.

stone ______________ nest ______________

step ______________

5. Write the list word that is the opposite of these.

sit ______________

stop ______________

found ______________

My List

____

____

____

____

____

clubhouse

Word Chain

1. Collect strips of paper.
2. Write a spelling word on each strip.
3. Join to make a word chain.

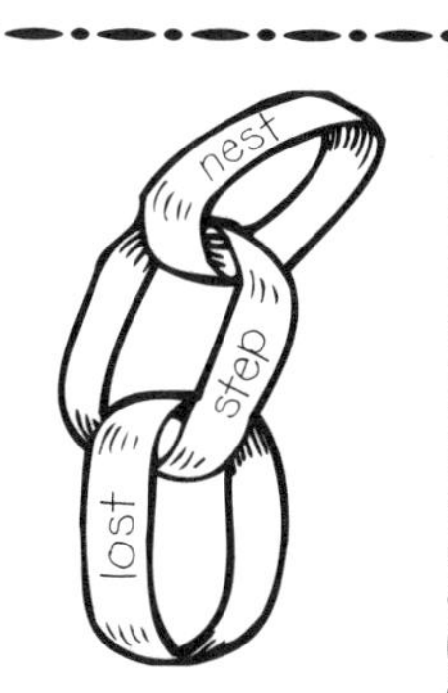

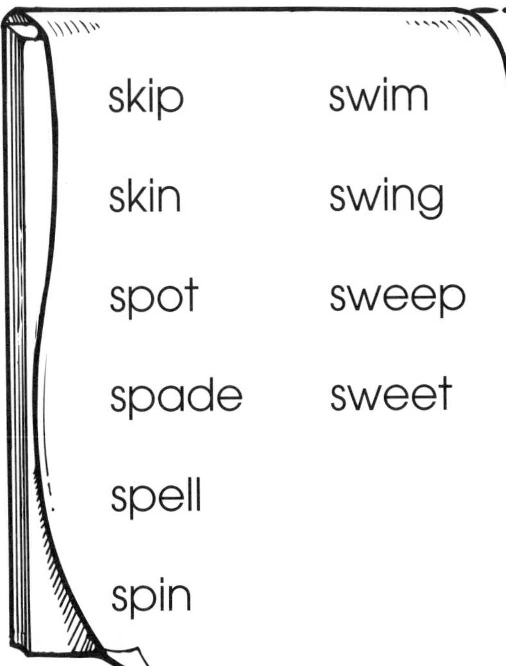

Look at the words.
Say each word.
Underline the pattern.

The words begin with s ☐, *s* ☐ *and s* ☐.

1. Write the correct beginning for each list word.

____ ____ eet ____ ____ ip

____ ____ ade ____ ____ im

____ ____ in ____ ____ ell

____ ____ ot ____ ____ in

____ ____ eep

____ ____ ing

3. Write the correct list word next to each picture.

____

____

____

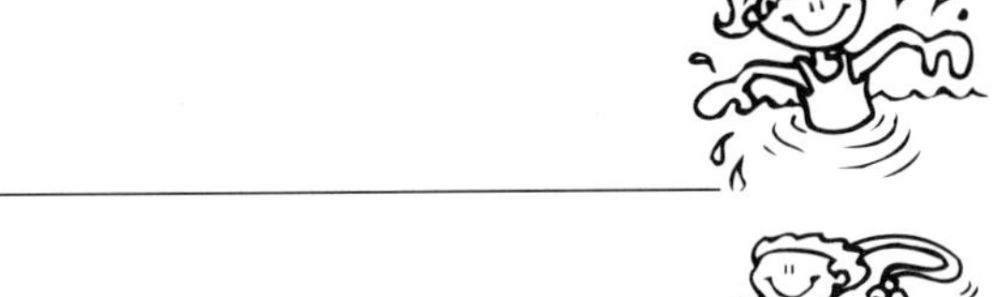
____

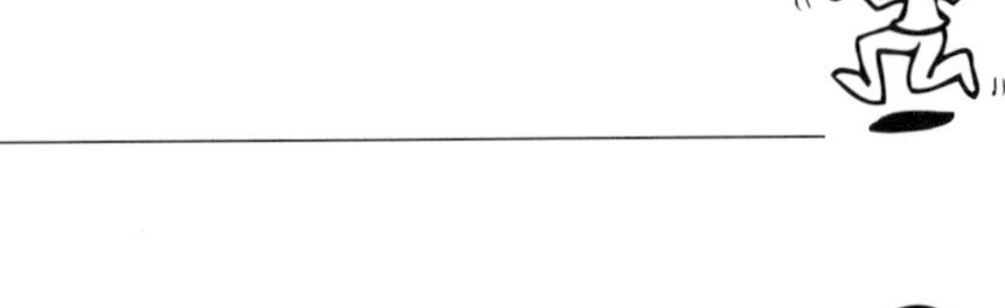
____

____

2. Which list words rhyme? ____________________ and ____________________

1. Write the **List Seven** words using – look, say, cover, write, check.
2. Find small words in skin, spot, spade, spin, swing, sweep and sweet.
3. Write **My List** words using – look, say, cover, write, check.
4. Sort **My List** words from easiest to hardest to spell.

Look how "ing" is added to the words below.

*jump – jump**ing***	*Only "ing" needs to be added.*
*run – run**ning***	*The last letter is doubled.*

4. Add "ing" to the list words below.

Only "ing" is added. sweep spell swing	Last letter is doubled. swim spin skip
____________	____________
____________	____________
____________	____________

5. Write a list word that means almost the same.

dot ____________

shovel ____________

turn ____________

sugar ____________

clubhouse

Word Ladder

1. Collect blank flashcards.
2. Write a spelling word on each card.
3. Join the cards with string to make a word ladder.

skip

spot

spin

tent	camp
spent	lamp
ant	jump
hint	bump
plant	lump

Look at the words.
Say each word.
Underline the pattern.

The pattern is  *and*

 *at the end of each word.*

1. Write the correct ending for each list word.

ju ____ ____

pla ____ ____

ca ____ ____ lu ____ ____

hi ____ ____ te ____ ____

bu ____ ____ a ____ ____

spe ____ ____ la ____ ____

2. Secret Words

Take "b" off bent and put in "t."

____

Take "u" off hunt and put in "i."

____

Take "st" off stamp and put in "l."

____

Take "d" off spend and put in "t."

____

Add "t" to the end of plan.

____

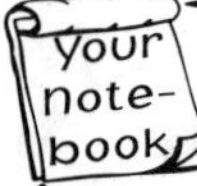

1. Write the **List Eight** words using – look, say, cover, write, check.
2. Sort the list words into those with three, four and five letters.
3. Write **My List** words using – look, say, cover, write, check.
4. Make word a shape for each **My List** word.

3. Unjumble the sentences. Circle the List Eight words.

(a) you slept tent? Have a in

____

(b) the on lamp. Turn

____

(c) cents. spent ten I

____

(d) ant An legs. has six

____

4. Add "ed" to these list words.

camp ______________

hint ______________

jump ______________

bump ______________

My List

____

____

____

____

____

clubhouse

Colorful Words

1. Write the **List Eight** words using two favorite colors to show the two patterns.
2. Write **My List** words using another color to show the tricky parts.

meat	near
teach	fear
beach	keep
leave	sleep
dear	sheet

Look at the words.
Say each word.
Underline the pattern.

The words have ☐☐,
☐☐☐ *or* ☐☐.

1. **Use "ee," "ea," or "ear" to complete these list words.**

sl ___ ___ p

n ___ ___ ___

sh ___ ___ t

m ___ ___ t

t ___ ___ ch

l ___ ___ ve

k ___ ___ p

d ___ ___ ___

f ___ ___ ___

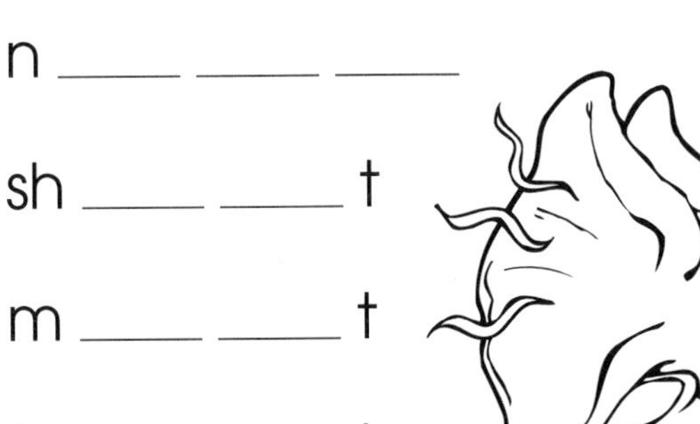

2. **Word Hunt**
Find another list word that rhymes.

teach ________________

keep ________________

meat ________________

Which three list words rhyme? ________________

____

____

Which list words end with the same last four letters?

____

____

your notebook

1. Write the **List Nine** words using – look, say, cover, write, check.
2. Write two more words with "ee." Do the same for "ea" and "ear."
3. Write **My List** words using – look, say, cover, write, check.
4. Write a rhyming word for each **My List** word.

3. Use the List Nine words to complete the sentences.

   (a) Put the chair ____________ the table.

   (b) I get ten hours of ____________ each night.

   (c) Do you ____________ your desk neat?

   (d) We ____________ for school at half past eight.

4. The words in the boxes sound alike but are spelled differently. Draw a picture to show each meaning.

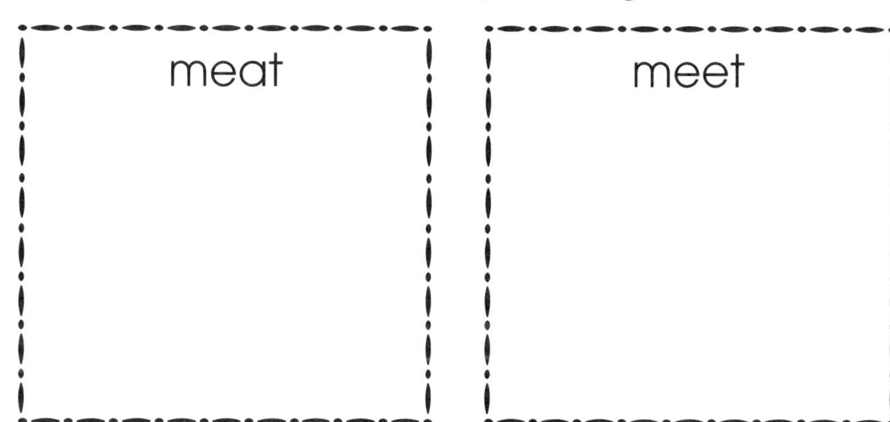

5. Add "er" to teach.

   ____

7. Add "es" to beach.

   ____

6. Write a list word that means almost the same.

   close ____________

   nap ____________

   scared ____________

clubhouse

Spiral Words

1. Draw a spiral on a sheet of paper.
2. Write words from both lists in the spiral.
3. Cut it out to make a word spiral. Hang it in your classroom.

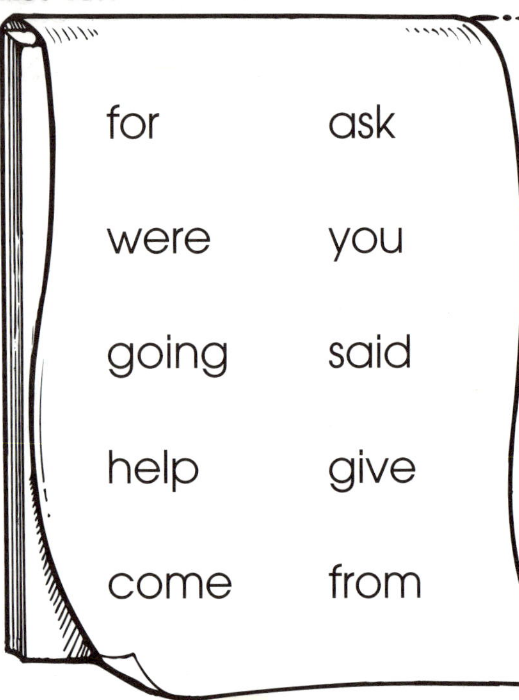

Look at the words.
Say each word.
Underline the tricky part.

2. Guess the list word by its shape.

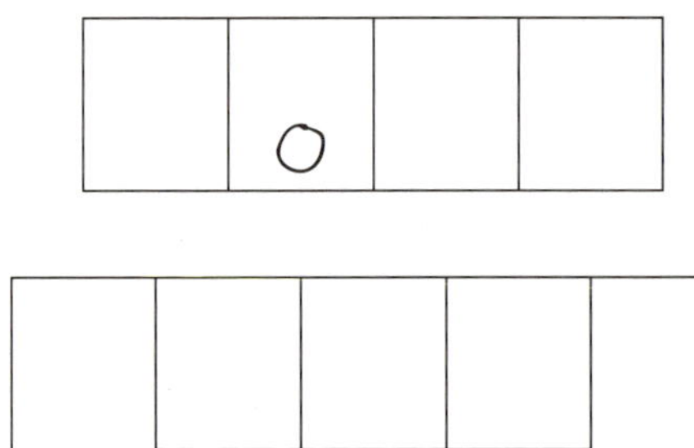

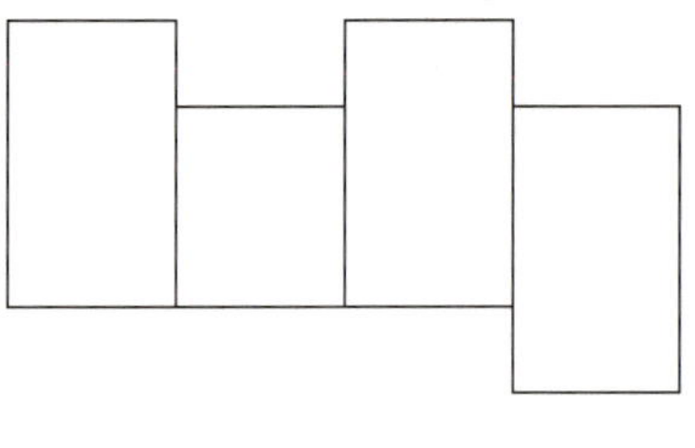

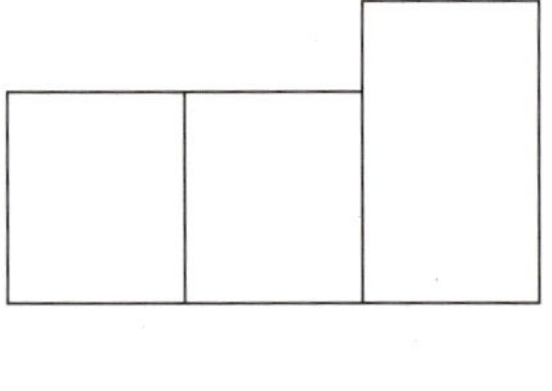

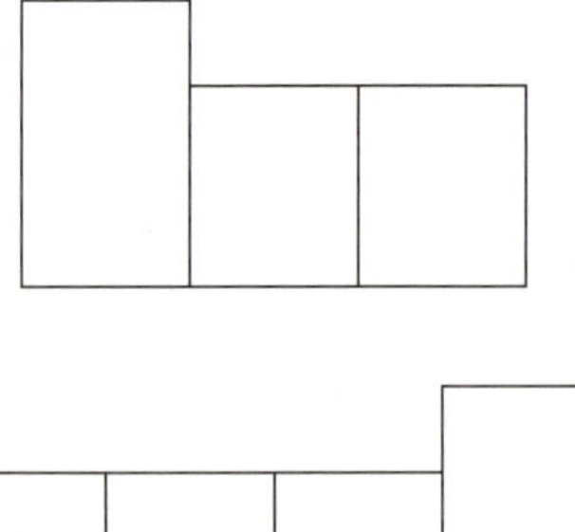

1. Fill in the missing letters to complete the list words.

h ___ lp   ___ ___ ing

___ ___ om   s ___ ___ d

w ___ r ___   g ___ v ___

a ___ ___   f ___ ___

y ___ ___   c ___ m ___

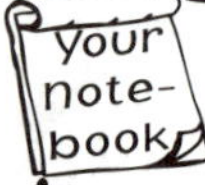

1. Write the **List Ten** words using – look, say, cover, write, check.
2. Sort the **List Ten** words from easiest to hardest to spell.
3. Write **My List** words using – look, say, cover, write, check.
4. Make spelling problems for each **My List** word. For example, f + or = for.

3. Choose the correct List Ten word.

(a) Please (going, give, help)

__________ each child a red pencil.

(b) My sister will take the dog (came, from, for) __________ a walk.

(c) A chicken comes (for, from, were) __________ an egg.

(d) "Would (give, ask, you) __________ like a slice of cake?" asked Mom.

4. Fill in the blanks.

said

sai ___

sa ___ ___

s ___ ___ ___

___ ___ ___ ___

5. Add "ed" to these list words.

ask __________

help __________

Make a Bookmark

1. Use cardboard to make a bookmark.
2. Write the words from each list on the bookmark.
3. Decorate your bookmark.

bang	sing
hang	thing
sang	being
song	sung
along	hung

Look at the words.
Say each word.
Underline the pattern.

The words end in ☐☐☐, ☐☐☐, ☐☐☐ *and* ☐☐☐.

1. **Write the correct ending for each list word.**

th ___ ___ ___

b ___ ___ ___

s ___ ___ ___

al ___ ___ ___

be ___ ___ ___

h ___ ___ ___

s ___ ___ ___

s ___ ___ ___

h ___ ___ ___

s ___ ___ ___

2. **Word Hunt**

Which list words rhyme with "rang"?

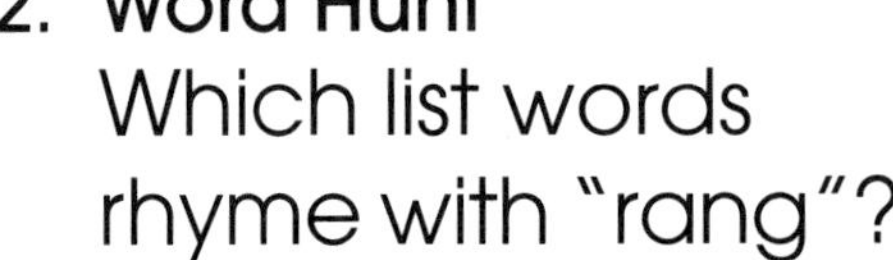

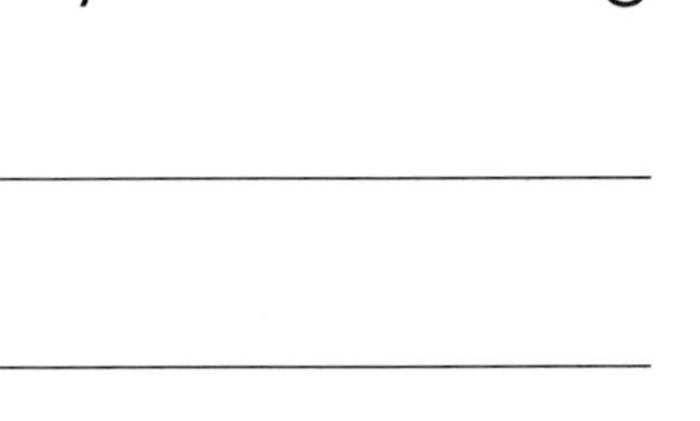

____

____

____

Which list words have five letters?

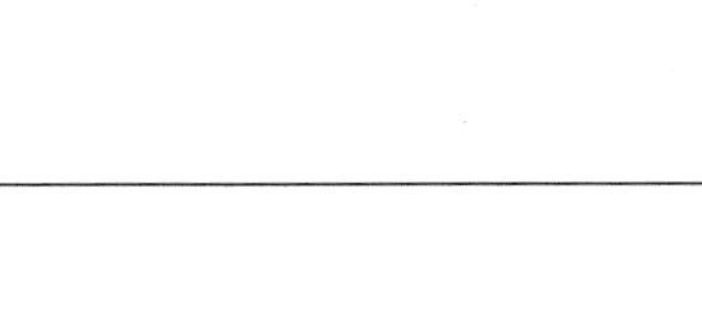

____

____

____

Which list words begin with "h"?

______________________ ______________________

1. Write the **List Eleven** words using – look, say, cover, write, check.
2. Write two more words that end with "ing." Do the same with "ang," "ong" and "ung."
3. Write **My List** words using – look, say, cover, write, check.
4. Write the **My List** words in alphabetical order.

3. Add "er" to these list words. Complete the sentences.

sing ______ A person who sings is a ____________________ .

hang ______ We use a ____________________ to hang clothes.

A compound word is made by joining two words together. For example, a + long = along.

4. Which words can you put before "thing" to make a new word?

Circle them. Write them on the lines.

any every

no **thing** yes

all some

____

____

____

____

5. Find small words in these.

being ________ ________

thing ________ ________

song ________ ________

My List

____

____

____

____

____

clubhouse

Pipe Cleaner Words

Use pipe cleaners to make the words from both lists.

sing

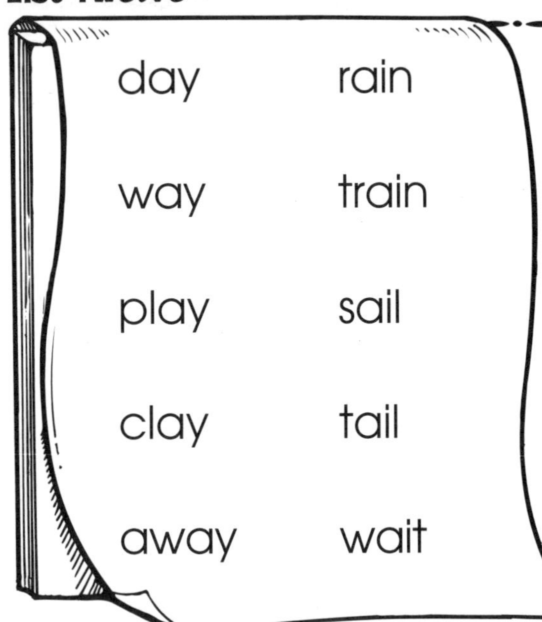

Look at the words.
Say each word.
Each word has the same sound.
Underline the sound.
The sound can be made by

☐☐ *or* ☐☐.

1. Use "ay" or "ai" to complete the list words.

w ____ ____ t   pl ____ ____

cl ____ ____   t ____ ____ l

tr ____ ____ n   d ____ ____

aw ____ ____   w ____ ____

s ____ ____ l   r ____ ____ n

2. Use the letters below to complete each puzzle. Cross out each letter as you use it.

a y y w l i

s d
a

t c r w i a a i

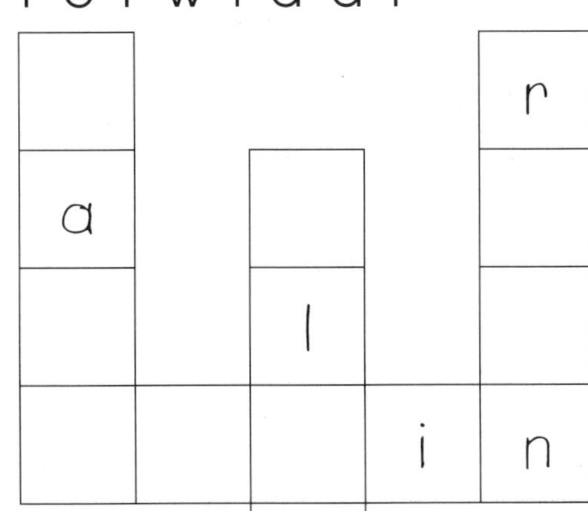

Your notebook

1. Write the **List Twelve** words using – look, say, cover, write, check.
2. Write a rhyming word for each **List Twelve** word.
3. Write **My List** words using – look, say, cover, write, check.
4. Write each **My List** word in a sentence.

Some words sound alike but have different spellings and meanings. They are called ***homophones.*** *For example, meat and meet.*

3. Draw a picture to show the meaning of one word from each pair. Circle the words you choose.

tail
tale

sail
sale

4. Choose the correct word from above to complete each sentence.

(a) A rabbit has a fluffy ______________ .

(b) You can buy things for less money at a ______________ .

(c) Another word for a story is a ______________ .

(d) We like to watch the boats ______________ on the river.

5. Add "ed" to these list words.

play ______________

wait ______________

rain ______________

sail ______________

clubhouse

Accordion Words

1. Fold long strips of paper like an accordion.
2. Write the words from both lists on the strips.
3. Cut the strips at the end of each word.

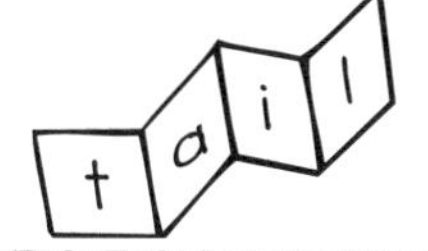

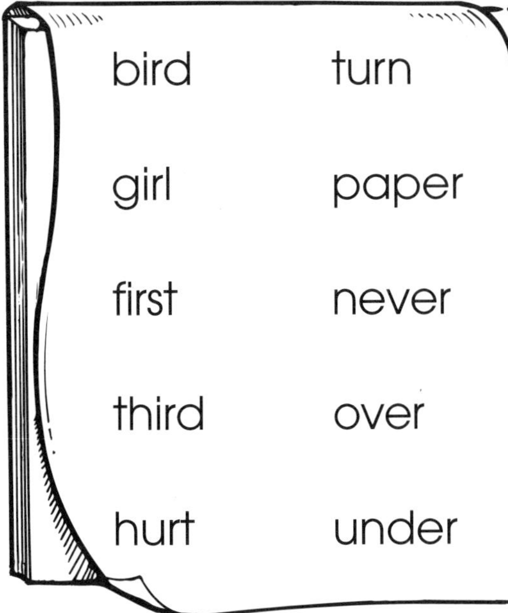

Look at the words.
Say each word.
Each word has the same sound.
Underline the sound.
The sound can be made by

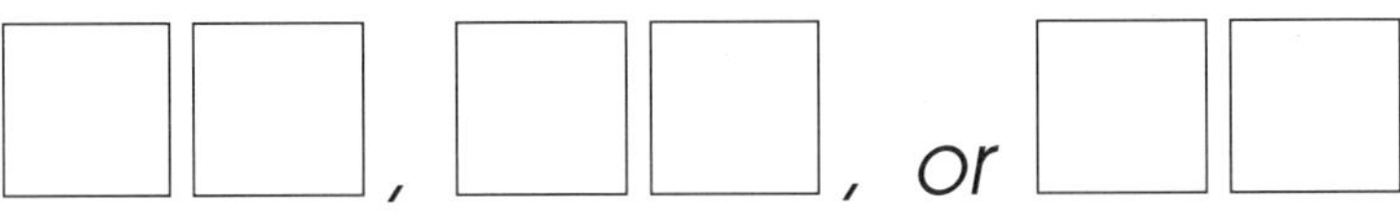

, , or .

1. Use "ir," "ur," or "er" to complete the list words.

h ___ ___ t   t ___ ___ n

th ___ ___ d   f ___ ___ st

ov ___ ___   pap ___ ___

nev ___ ___   und ___ ___

g ___ ___ l   b ___ ___ d

2. Secret Words

Add "n" to the start of ever.

____

Take "b" off burn
and put in "t."

____

Take "th" off thunder.

____

Take "wh" off whirl
and put in "g."

____

Take "n" off oven
and put in "r."

____

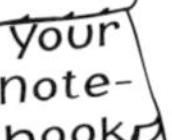

1. Write the **List Thirteen** words using – look, say, cover, write, check.
2. Choose five **List Thirteen** words and write each in a sentence.
3. Write **My List** words using – look, say, cover, write, check.
4. Make a word shape for each **My List** word.

3. Find a List Thirteen word that is the opposite of the word in parentheses to complete the sentences.

   (a) I came (last) ____________ in my race.

   (b) The cow jumped (under) ____________ the moon.

   (c) She is (always) ____________ late for school.

   (d) We drove (over) ____________ the bridge.

> *Words can be broken into **syllables** or word parts.*
> *This can help us spell words.*
> *For example, **away** has two syllables – **a** and **way**.*

4. Sort these list words into one or two syllables.

   girl under paper bird over never first hurt

One syllable	Two syllables

clubhouse

Colorful Words

1. Write **List Thirteen** words using three favorite colors to show the three patterns.
2. Write **My List** words using another color to show the tricky parts.

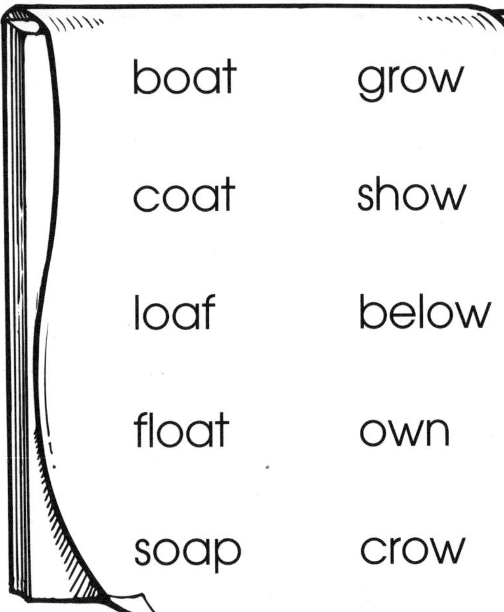

Look at the words.
Say each word.
Each word has the same sound.
Underline the sound.
The sound can be made by

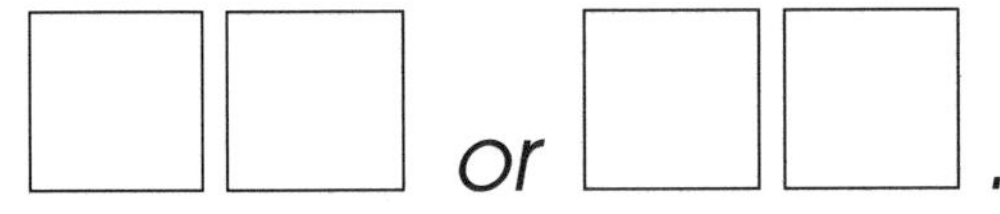
or .

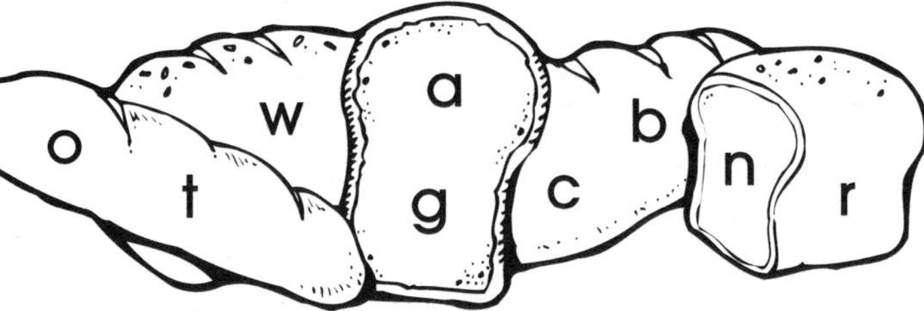

1. Use "oa" or "ow" to complete the list words.

bel ____ ____

____ ____ n

s ____ ____ p

l ____ ____ f

b ____ ____ t

cr ____ ____

sh ____ ____

gr ____ ____

fl ____ ____ t

c ____ ____ t

2. Write five list words using the letters on the bread.

____

____

____

____

____

3. What list words are the opposite of these?

above ______________________

sink ______________________

1. Write the **List Fourteen** words using – look, say, cover, write, check.
2. Make spelling problems for the **List Fourteen** words. For example, b + oat = boat.
3. Write **My List** words using – look, say, cover, write, check.
4. Sort the **My List** words from easiest to hardest to spell.

4. Answer yes or no. Circle the list words.

   (a) Does soap help make you clean? ______________

   (b) Can trees grow below the ground? ______________

   (c) Can a boat float on land? ______________

   (d) Do you own a pet crow? ______________

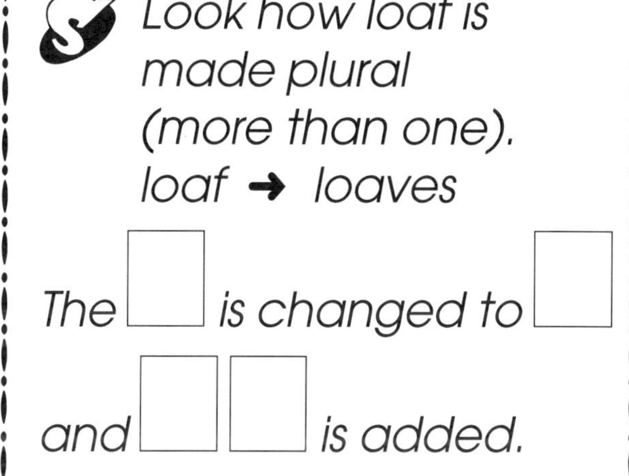

Look how loaf is made plural (more than one).

loaf ➜ loaves

The ☐ *is changed to* ☐

and ☐ ☐ *is added.*

5. The word "floating" is made from "float." From which list words have these words been made? Circle the letters that have been added.

showing ______________

coats ______________

owned ______________

grown ______________

floated ______________

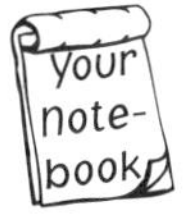

6. Write a sentence for loaf and another sentence for loaves.

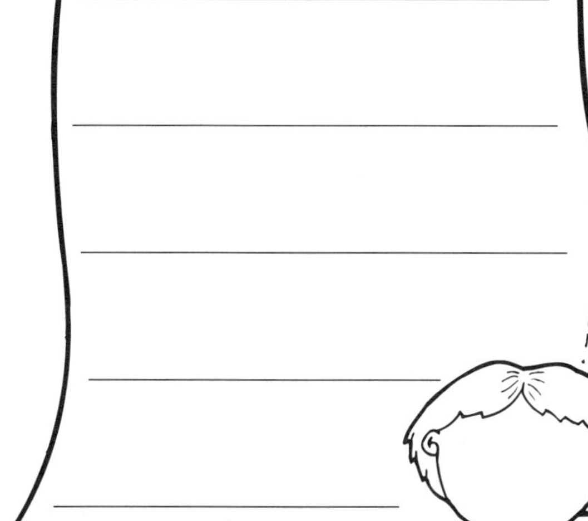

Word Chain

1. Make strips of paper.
2. Write a spelling word on each strip.
3. Join to make a word chain.

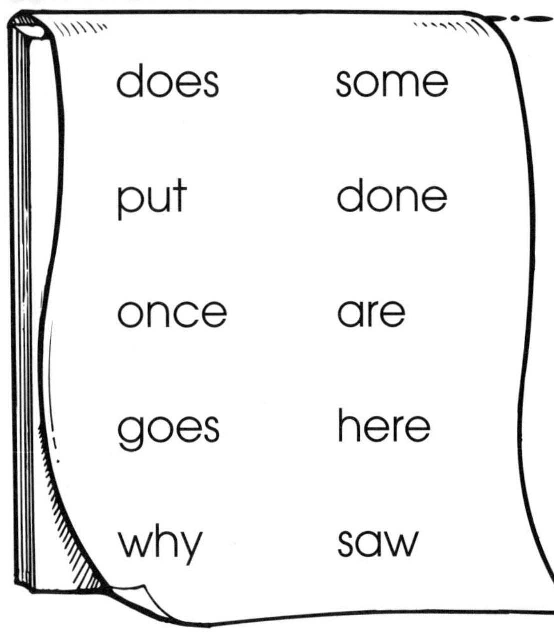

Look at the words.
Say each word.
Underline the tricky part.

2. Guess the list word by its shape.

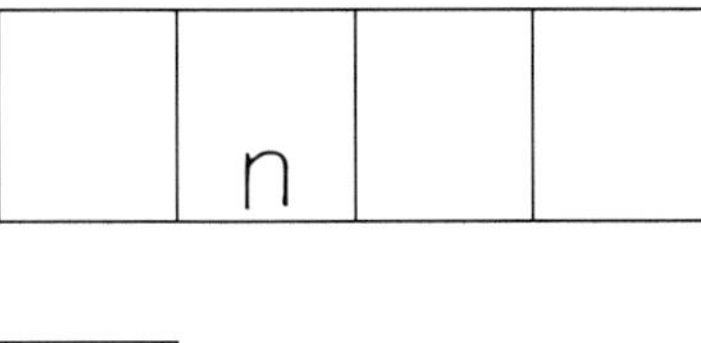

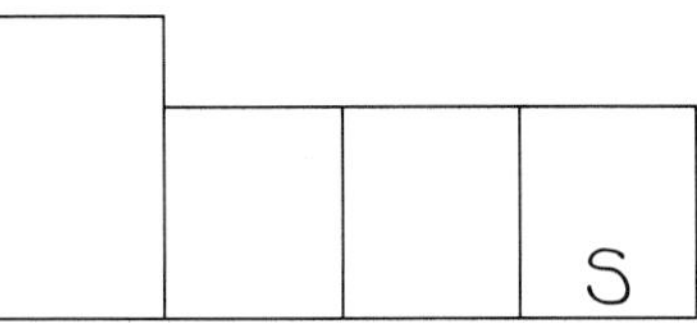

1. Fill in the missing letters to complete the list words.

___ ___ e h ___ r ___

p ___ t g ___ ___ s

s ___ ___ d ___ ___ s

___ ___ y s ___ m ___

___ ___ ce d ___ n ___

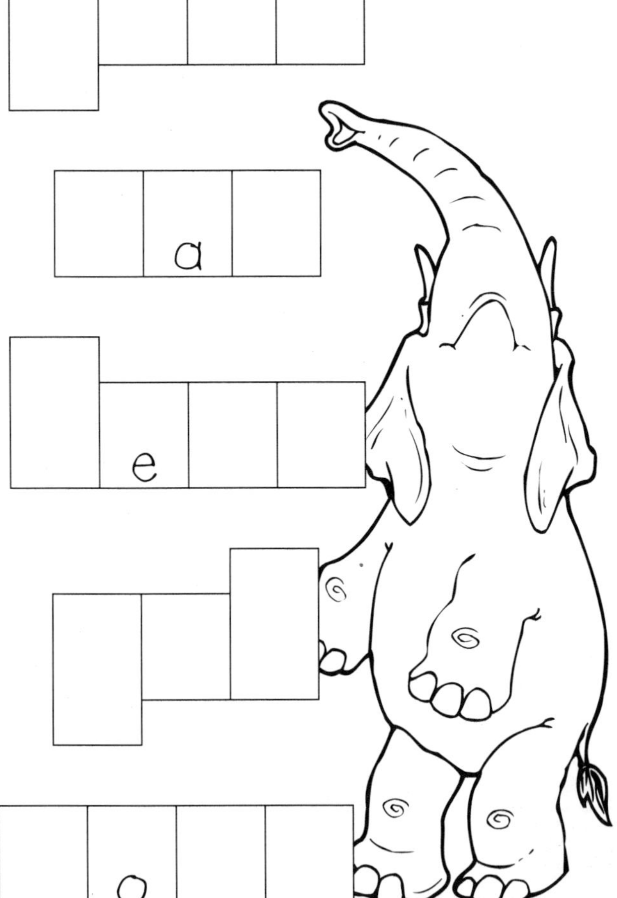

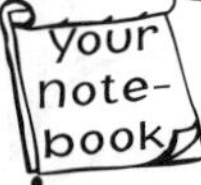

1. Write the **List Fifteen** words using – look, say, cover, write, check.
2. Sort the list words from easiest to hardest to spell.
3. Write **My List** words using – look, say, cover, write, check.
4. Write a rhyming word for each **My List** word.

3. The missing list words are at the beginning of each sentence. Remember to use a capital letter.

(a) ____________________ were you late for school?

(b) ____________________ the book on the table.

(c) ____________________ you going to Jane's party?

(d) ____________________ your dog sleep in a kennel?

The words "here" and "hear" are ***homophones****. They sound alike but have different spellings and meanings.*

4. Write a sentence for "here." Draw a picture for "hear."

____

____

5. Fill in the blanks.

saw

sa ____

s ____ ____

____ ____ ____

clubhouse

Word Mobile

Make a mobile of the **List Fifteen** and **My List** words.

saw some does here once

My List

____

____

____

____

____

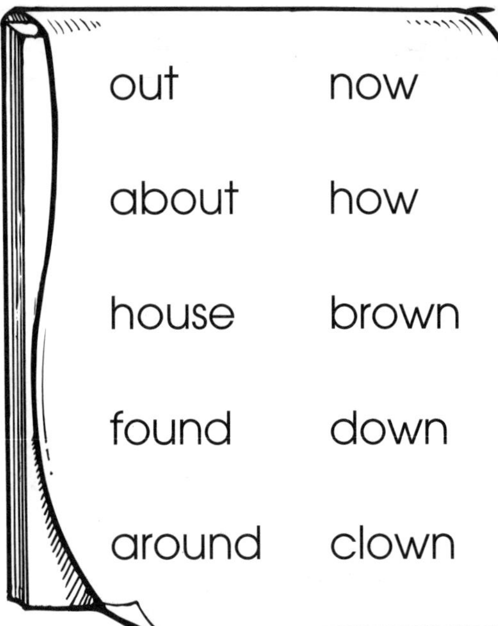

Look at the words.
Say each word.
Each word has the same sound.
Underline the sound.
The sound can be made by

☐☐ *or* ☐☐.

1. Use "ou" or "ow" to complete the list words.

___ ___ t   n ___ ___

d ___ ___ n   h ___ ___

f ___ ___ nd

cl ___ ___ n

ar ___ ___ nd

ab ___ ___ t

br ___ ___ n

h ___ ___ se

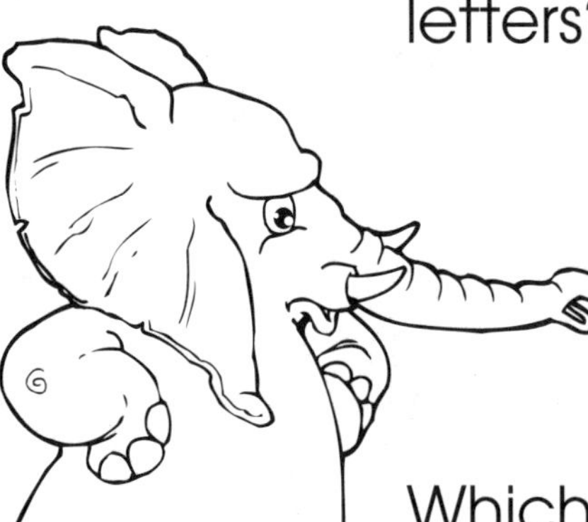

2. Word Hunt

Which list words rhyme with "frown"?

____

____

____

Which list words have three letters?

____

____

____

Which list words have the same last four letters?

____

____

Your note-book

1. Write the **List Sixteen** words using look, say, cover, write, check.
2. Write three more "ou" words. Do the same for "ow." Check the spelling.
3. Write **My List** words using – look, say, cover, write, check.
4. Make spelling problems for each **My List** word. For example, ou + t = out.

3. Unjumble the sentences. Circle the List Sixteen words.

(a) clown The shoes. has brown

____

(b) ladder. down Climb the

____

(c) do How it? you do

____

(d) around the Run tree.

____

4. Which List Sixteen words have two syllables?

____________________ ____________________

5. Write the list word that is the opposite of each of these.

up ____________________

in ____________________

lost ____________________

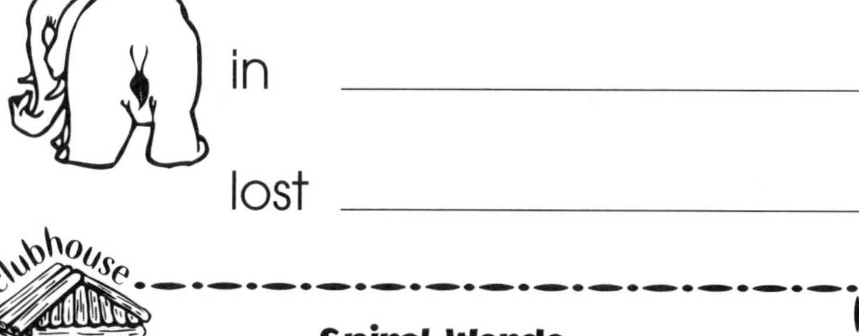

Spiral Words

1. Draw a spiral on a sheet of paper.
2. Write words from both lists in the spiral.
3. Cut it out to make a word spiral. Hang it in your classroom.

Look at the words.
Say each word.
Underline the pattern.

The words end in ☐.

1. Write the correct ending to complete the list words.

bun ___ ___ sto ___ ___

hap ___ ___ par ___ ___

ve ___ ___ fun ___ ___

la ___ ___ on ___ ___

sil ___ ___ ba ___ ___

2. Use the letters below to complete the puzzle. Cross out each letter as you use it.

y v i s o l n r

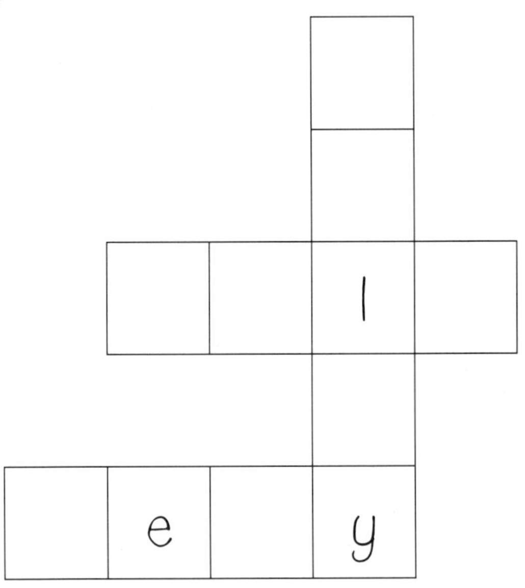

3. Which list words rhyme?

____

____

4. Complete the list word.

___ a ___ y

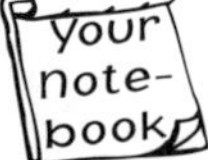

1. Write the **List Seventeen** words using – look, say, cover, write, check.
2. Sort the **List Seventeen** words into those with four and five letters.
3. Write **My List** words using – look, say, cover, write, check.
4. Write the **My List** words in alphabetical order.

5. Find small words in these.

story ______________ party ______________

funny ______________ only ______________

bunny ______________

Look at these words.
*One body – two bod**ies***
The "y" is changed to "i"
Then "es" is added.

6. Do the same to these list words.

baby ______________

party ______________

story ______________

lady ______________

bunny ______________

7. Write a list word that means the same.

woman

____

tale

____

tot

____

My List

____

____

____

____

____

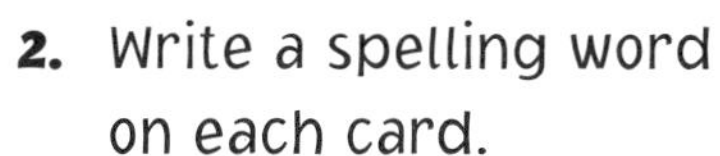

Make a Jigsaw Puzzle

1. Collect blank flashcards.
2. Write a spelling word on each card.
3. Cut each card into a jigsaw puzzle.

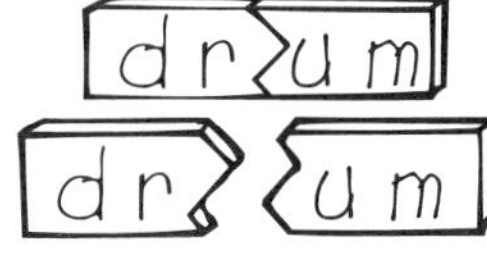

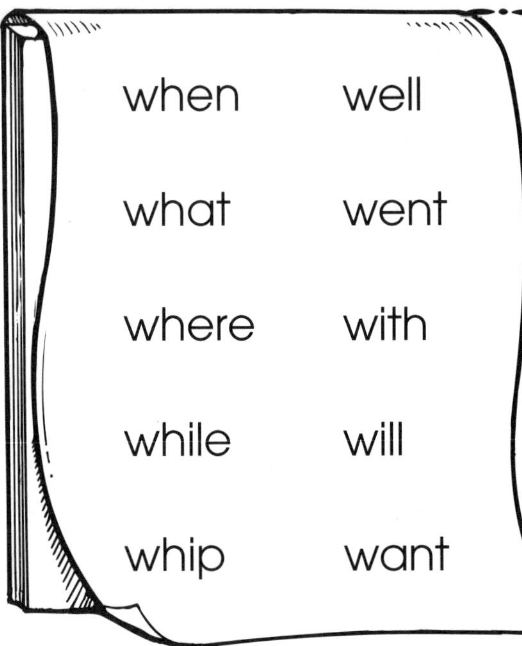

Look at the words.
Say each word.
Underline the patterns.

The words begin with ☐☐

or ☐.

1. **Use "wh" or "w" to complete each list word.**

___ ent　　___ ___ ile

___ ill　　___ ___ ere

___ ell　　___ ith

___ ___ en　　___ ___ at

___ ant　　___ ___ ip

2. **Secret Words**

Take "sp" off spell and put in "w."

____

Take "sm" off smile and put in "wh."

____

Take "ed" from wanted.

____

Take "s" off ship and put in "w."

____

Take "a" from whale and put in "i."

____

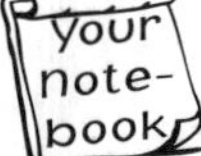

1. Write the **List Eighteen** words using – look, say, cover, write, check.
2. Make spelling problems for the **List Eighteen** words. For example, wh + en = when.
3. Write **My List** words using – look, say, cover, write, check.
4. Write each **My List** word in a sentence.

3. The missing list words are at the beginning of each sentence. Remember to use a capital letter. Answer the questions.

(a) ______ is your name? ______

(b) ______ do you live? ______

______

(c) ______ is your birthday? ______

______

4. Find small words in these.

where ______

when ______

what ______

want ______

will ______

My List

______

______

______

______

______

clubhouse

Make a Bookmark

1. Use cardboard to make a bookmark.
2. Write the words from each list onto the bookmark.
3. Decorate your bookmark.

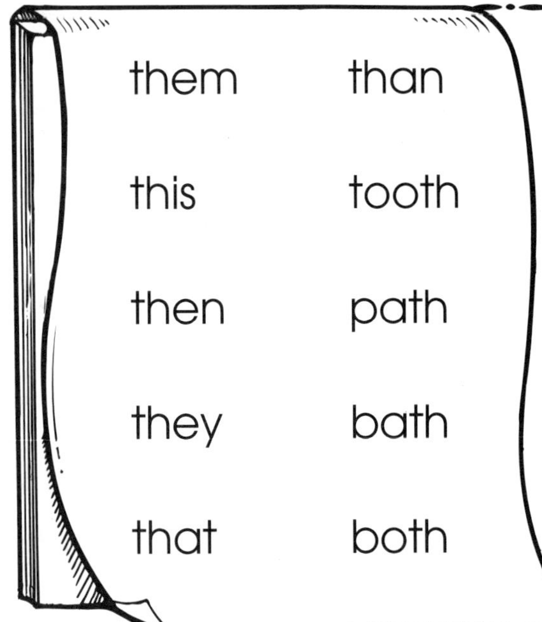

Look at the words.
Say each word.
Underline the pattern.
The words begin or end

with ☐☐.

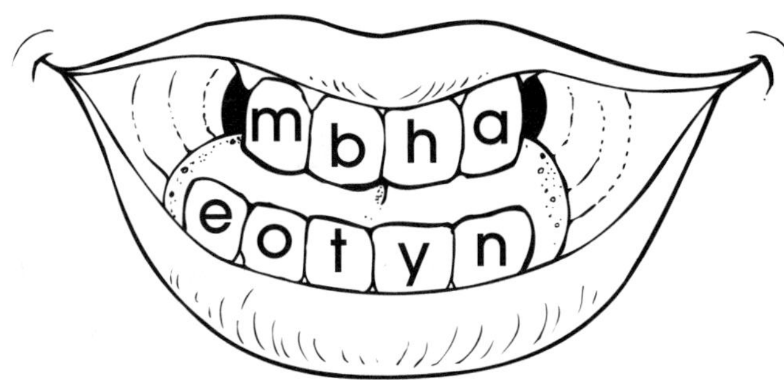

1. Fill in the missing vowels to complete each list word.

th ___ y　　th ___ m 

b ___ th　　th ___ n

th ___ t

p ___ th

b ___ th

th ___ n

th ___ s

t ___ ___ th

2. Find six list words using the letters in the smile. Use each letter only once in the same word.

____

____

____

____

____

____

3. Find a list word that means the same.

trail ______________________

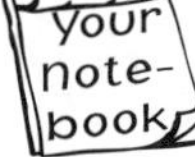

1. Write the **List Nineteen** words using – look, say, cover, write, check.
2. Sort the **List Nineteen** words from easiest to hardest to spell.
3. Write **My List** words using – look, say, cover, write, check.
4. Make word shapes for each **My List** word.

4. Choose the correct word.

   (a) We give our dog a (bath, baths) ____________ every two weeks.

   (b) It is safer to ride on a bicycle (path, paths) ____________ .

   (c) Did you remember to brush your (tooth, teeth) ____________ ?

5. Write these words in alphabetical order.

   then both path tooth

   ____

   ____

   ____

   ____

6. Find a list word that rhymes.

   miss ____________

   stay ____________

   flat ____________

7. Say these words aloud.

   them bath

   them has a hard "th"
   bath has a soft "th"

   Put a check mark next to the hard "th" words in the list.

   Put a circle around the soft "th" words in the list.

clubhouse

Colorful Words

1. Choose three favorite colors.
2. Use one color to write both lists of words.
3. Trace around the words with the other two colors.

Look at the words.
Say each word.
These words are contractions.

An ☐ (apostrophe) is put in where the letters have been left out.

1. Write the correct list word.

cannot = ____________ is not = ____________

we are = ____________ she is = ____________

I am = ____________ do not = ____________

he is = ____________ it is = ____________

I have = ____________ I will = ____________

2. Put the ' (apostrophe) in the correct place.

were its isnt Ive

hes shes cant dont

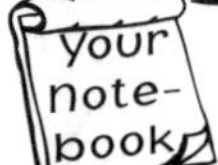

1. Write the **List Twenty** words using – look, say, cover, write, check.
2. Write five more contractions.
3. Write **My List** words using – look, say, cover, write, check.
4. Sort the **My List** words from easiest to hardest to spell.

3. Sort the List Twenty words into family groups.

n't	's	'm	'll
don't			
		're	**'ve**

4. Circle the letters that will be left out to make the contraction. Write the contraction.

I have = I've

do not =

he is =

we are =

she is =

is not =

cannot =

it is =

I am =

I will =

clubhouse

Word Ladder

1. Collect blank flashcards.
2. Write a spelling word on each card.
3. Join the cards with string to make a word ladder.

he's
don't
she's

List One - Page 16
1. Teacher check
2. Word Hunt: rhyming words – wish, dish, fish
five letters – sheep, brush, smash
four letters/end in "p" – ship, shop

Page 17
3. hip, hop, hut, in, she, he
4. (a) shut (b) sheep (c) fish (d) ship
5. ships, shops, shins
6. wishes, dishes, brushes

List Two - Page 18
1. Teacher check
2. chop, rich, much, such, each, chip
3. chin, lunch

Page 19
4. (a) such (b) each (c) much (d) chick
5. chicks, lunches, chest
6. hop, hip, in

List Three - Page 20
1. Teacher check
2. came, like, five, gave, made
3. kite

Page 21
4. (a) **Take** the book with you.
(b) Can you **ride** a bike?
(c) What is the **time**?
(d) I can **make** my bed.
5. making, riding, timing

List Four - Page 22
1. Teacher check
2. Word Hunt: shortest word – use
longest word – those
rhyming words – tube, cube
same meaning – home, tube

Page 23
3. (a) cute (b) woke (c) bone (d) note
4. use**d**, note**s**, woke**n**, cube**s**, us**ing** (use)

List Five - Page 24
1. Teacher check
2. drip, crib, bring, brave, try

Page 25
3. (a) trip (b) drum (c) grubs (d) Crabs
4. tries, dries, fries, flies
5. Teacher check

List Six - Page 26
1. Teacher check
2. stop, stone, step, nest, must, lost

Page 27
3. (a) stop (b) stopped (c) start (d) started
4. stones, nests, steps
5. stand, start, lost

List Seven - Page 28
1. Teacher check
2. spin, skin
3. swing, sweep, spade, swim, skip, spot

Your Notebook
2. skin – kin, in; spot – pot; spade – pad, spa, a; spin – pin, in; swing – wing, win, in; sweep – weep, wee, we; sweet – wee, we

Page 29
4. sweeping, spelling, swinging swimming, spinning, skipping
5. spot, spade, spin, sweet

List Eight - Page 30
1. Teacher check
2. tent, hint, lamp, spent, plant

Your Notebook
2. three letters – ant; four letters – tent, hint, camp, lamp, jump, bump, lump; five letters – spent, plant

Page 31
3. (a) Have you slept in a **tent**?
(b) Turn on the **lamp**.
(c) I **spent** ten cents.
(d) An **ant** has six legs.
4. camped, hinted, jumped, bumped, planted

List Nine - Page 32
1. Teacher check
2. Word Hunt:
rhyming words – beach, sleep, sheet
three rhyming words – dear, near, fear
same last four letters – teach, beach

Page 33
3. (a) near (b) sleep (c) keep (d) leave
4. Teacher check
5. teacher
6. near, sleep, fear
7. beaches

List Ten - Page 34
1. Teacher check
2. come, going, were, help, ask, for, said

Page 35
3. (a) give (b) for (c) from (d) you
4. Teacher check
5. asked, helped

List Eleven - Page 36
1. Teacher check
2. Word Hunt: rhyming – bang, hang, sang
five letters – being, thing, along
begin with "h" – hang, hung

Page 37
3. singer, hanger
4. anything, everything, something, nothing
5. be, in; thin, in; so, son, on

List Twelve - Page 38
1. Teacher check
2. sail, day, away; wait, clay, rain, train

Page 39
3. Teacher check
4. (a) tail (b) sale (c) tale (d) sail
5. played, waited, rained, sailed

List Thirteen - Page 40
1. Teacher check
2. never, turn, under, girl, over

Page 41
3. (a) first (b) over (c) never (d) under
4. one syllable – girl, bird, first, hurt
two syllables – under, paper, over, never

List Fourteen - Page 42
1. Teacher check
2. boat, coat, grow, own, crow
3. below, float

Page 43
4. Teacher check
5. show**ing**, coat**s**, own**ed**, grow**n**, float**ed**
6. Teacher check

List Fifteen - Page 44
1. Teacher check
2. once, does, goes, saw, here, put, some

Page 45
3. (a) Why (b) Put (c) Are (d) Does
4. Teacher check
5. Teacher check

List Sixteen - Page 46
1. Teacher check
2. Word Hunt:
rhyming words – brown, down, clown
three letters – out, now, how
same last four letters – found, around

Page 47
3. (a) The **clown** has **brown** shoes.
(b) Climb **down** the ladder.
(c) **How** do you do it?
(d) Run **around** the tree.
4. about, around
5. down, out, found

List Seventeen - Page 48
1. Teacher check 2. only, very, silly
3. bunny, funny 4. baby/lady

Your Notebook
2. Four letters – lady, baby, only, very
Five letters – story, party, happy, bunny, funny, silly

Page 49
5. to/or; fun; bun; part, art, a; on
6. babies, parties, stories, ladies, bunnies
7. lady, story, baby

List Eighteen - Page 50
1. Teacher check
2. well, while, want, whip, while

Page 51
3. (a) What (b) Where (c) When
4. here, her, he; hen, he; hat, at, a; ant, an, a; ill

List Nineteen - Page 52
1. Teacher check
2. them, then, they, both, bath, than
3. path

Page 53
4. (a) bath (b) path (c) teeth
5. both, path, then, tooth
6. this, they, that
7. hard "th" – them, this, then, they, that, than
soft "th" – both, tooth, path, bath

List Twenty - Page 54
1. Teacher check
2. Teacher check

Page 55
3. n't – don't, isn't, can't
's – he's, she's, it's
'm – I'm
'll – I'll
've – I've
're - we're
4. Teacher check

also	of
have	off
to	could
too	would
two	should

Look at the words.
Say each word.
Underline the tricky part.

1. Complete these list words.

sh ___ ___ ___ ___

___ a ___ e

___ w ___

c ___ ___ ___ ___

___ f ___

t ___

___ l ___ ___

o ___

___ oo

___ ou ___ ___

2. Match the word parts. Write the words you made.

co •	• ve	___
ha •	• so	___
of •	• ould	___
sh •	• uld	could
al •	• f	___

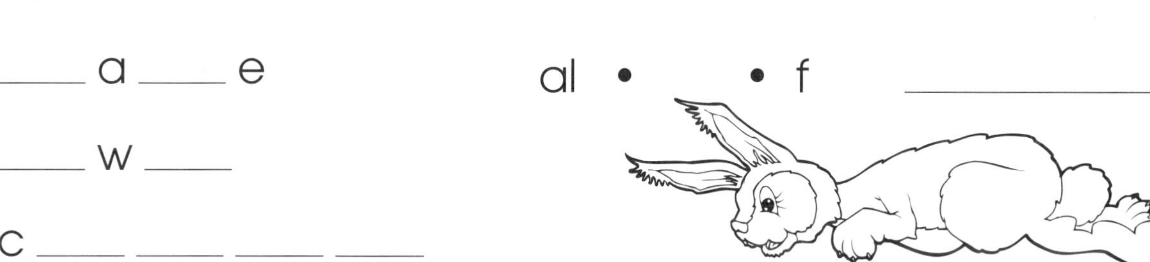

3. Find the hidden list words. Write them down.

___
___
___
___
___

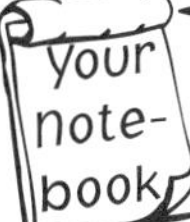

1. Write the **List One** words using - look, say, cover, write, check.
2. Jumble the **List One** words. Give them to a friend to unjumble.
3. Write **My List** words using - look, say, cover, write, check.
4. Make words shapes for **My List** words.

4. Complete these sentences using words from the list.

(a) "I ________ ________ many toys," complained Scott.

(b) It is important ________ turn water faucets ________ tightly.

(c) Mandy has ________ brothers ________ the same age.

5. Sort the list words according to the number of letters.

2 letters	3 letters	4 letters	5 letters	6 letters

6. Can you think of a homophone for would? Write the word and draw its picture.

____

> *To, too and two are all* ***homophones****. They sound the same but are spelled differently and have different meanings.*

7. Sort My List words according to the number of letters.

clubhouse

Jigsaw Puzzle

1. Collect 15 flashcards. Cut each one into two jigsaw pieces.
2. Write a spelling word across two pieces that match.
3. Ask a friend to put them together.

List Two **Spelling Success**

car	last
star	fast
part	class
harm	master
garden	basket

Look at the words.
Say each word.
Find the pattern for each column of words. The patterns are:

☐☐ *and* ☐☐.

Underline the patterns.

1. Complete these list words.

l ___ ___ ___

s ___ ___ ___

cl ___ ___ ___

m ___ ___ ___ er

h ___ ___ ___

b ___ ___ ___ et

p ___ ___ ___

f ___ ___ ___

g ___ ___ d ___ ___

c ___ ___

2. Write the spelling words which contain these small words.

art ________________

lass ________________

den ________________

arm ________________

mast ________________

ask ________________

tar ________________

3. Unjumble the three list words jumbled together.

a a a c f l r s s t t

____

________________ ________________

Your notebook

1. Write the **List Two** words using - look, say, cover, write, check.
2. Write the **List Two** words in alphabetical order.
3. Write **My List** words using – look, say, cover, write, check.
4. Use a dictionary to write a definition for each **My List** word.

4. Can you complete this grid?

word	"er"	"est"
tall		
small		
loud		
slow		

Antonyms *are words which mean the opposite. For example, hot and cold.*

5. Write the antonyms from the list for these words.

mistress ______________

slow ______________

first ______________

care ______________

whole ______________

7. How many compound words can you make using "star"?

light

fish **star** one

yes dust

______________ ______________

____

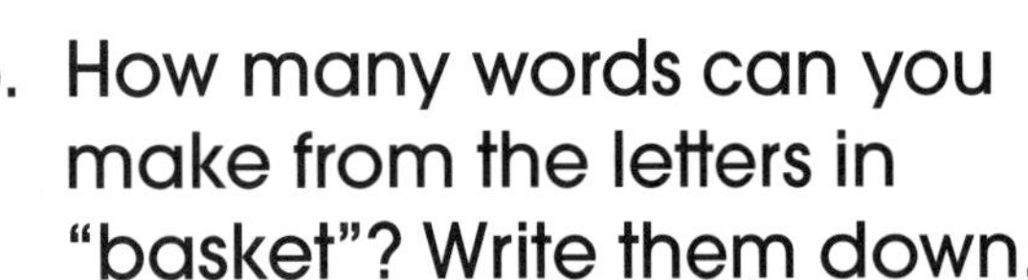

6. How many words can you make from the letters in "basket"? Write them down.

Picture Words

1. Draw a picture for each **List Two** and **My List** word on a separate piece of paper.
2. Write a sentence under each picture, highlighting each word.
3. Make a book out of the papers.

blew	due
chew	broomstick
grew	balloon
crew	bedroom
glue	spoon

Look at the words.
Say each word.
Each word has the same sound.
The sound can be made by

Underline the sound.

1. Complete these list words.

b ____ dr ____ ____ m

cr ____ ____

d ____ ____

b ____ ll ____ ____ n

gr ____ ____

sp ____ ____ n

gl ____ ____

ch ____ ____

br ____ ____ mst ____ ck

bl ____ ____

2. Sort the list words according to the number of letters.

3	
4	
5	
7	
10	

Your notebook

1. Write the **List Three** words using – look, say, cover, write, check.
2. Choose five **List Three** words and write each in a question.
3. Write **My List** words using – look, say, cover, write, check.
4. Write each **My List** word in an interesting sentence.

Homophones *are words that sound the same but have different meanings and different spellings. For example, due and dew.*

3. Circle the correct homophone for these pictures.

blue/blew | see/sea | son/sun

Sometimes two words can be joined together to make a new word. These words are called ***compound words****. For example, sun + light = sunlight.*

4. Can you make compound words from these?

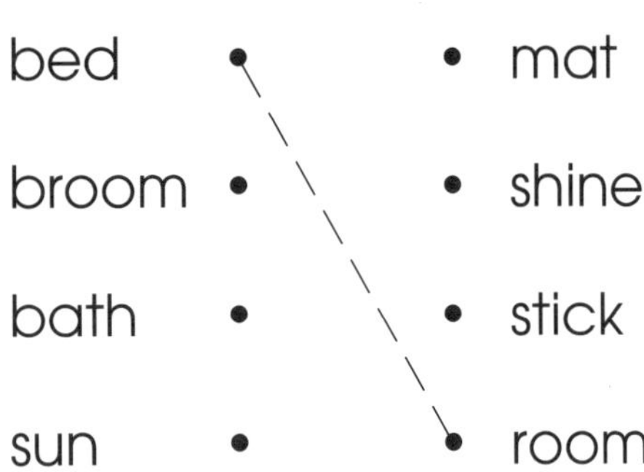

bed •	• mat	______
broom •	• shine	______
bath •	• stick	______
sun •	• room	bedroom

5. *A group of people, animals or objects are given a name to make it easier to refer to them. For example, a group of sailors is called a crew.*
What is a group of puppies called?

______

Draw a Plan

1. Draw a plan of your bedroom on paper.
2. Write the **List Three** words and **My List** words over the furniture.
3. Color and decorate using your favorite colors.

Picture Three 

Study this picture carefully–imagine you are a detective. Try to remember as many details as you can.

Question Sheet Three

Answer these questions related to Picture Three.

1. How many cushions was the girl leaning against? ______________________

2. What was the girl doing?

   ____

3. What was the picture on the wall showing?

   ____

4. Could you see the nail holding up the picture?

   ____

5. Did the girl have ribbons in her hair?

   ____

Challenge!

Which foot was on top of the other?

____

Picture Five 

Study this picture carefully–imagine you are a detective. Try to remember as many details as you can.

Question Sheet Five

Answer these questions related to Picture Five.

1. How many pillows could you see on the bed?

   ____

2. Were the numbers on the clock in black or white?

   ____

3. How many books were on the bedside table? ______________________________

4. Could you see one of the boy's ears?

   ____

5. How many knobs could you see on the bedside drawer?

   ____

Challenge!

Could you see the teddy's mouth above the bedclothes? ______________